PENGUIN BOOKS

Seasons in Tuscany

This book is a miscellany of reflections, musings, discoveries and experiences from a very important year in my life. As much as it is a love story, I hope it is also a history book and a cultural celebration of a very beautiful part of Europe. Where possible, I have tried to be historically and culturally accurate. But I have not laid an undue emphasis on this; rather I have tried to report on events, people, places and history as I observed, experienced or was told about them. There are bound to be errors of fact in the book. These are mine alone, as are my assessments of Italy, Tuscany and its people. I hope also that I have not offended anyone too deeply. That was not my aim. Again, my observations on the people I came in contact with are reflections of how I found them and how I reacted to them. The responsibility for these is mine alone.

Allan Parker
San Clemente
Trequanda
Tuscany

This book is for Stephen and Andrew, in the hope that one day they will understand. It is also for Terry and Diane, Dennis and Rhonda.

They know why.

But above all it is for Nancy.

Seasons in Tuscany

A tale of two loves

Allan Parker

PENGUIN BOOKS

PENGUIN BOOKS

Penguin Books (NZ) Ltd, cnr Airborne and Rosedale Roads, Albany,
Auckland 1310, New Zealand
Penguin Books Ltd, 27 Wrights Lane, London W8 5TZ, England
Penguin Putnam Inc, 375 Hudson Street, New York, NY 10014, United States
Penguin Books Australia Ltd, 487 Maroondah Highway, Ringwood, Australia 3134
Penguin Books Canada Ltd, 10 Alcorn Avenue, Toronto, Ontario, Canada M4V 3B2
Penguin Books (South Africa) Pty Ltd, 5 Watkins Street, Denver Ext 4, 2094, South Africa
Penguin Books India (P) Ltd, 11, Community Centre, Panchsheel Park,
New Delhi 110 017, India

Penguin Books Ltd, Registered Offices: Harmondsworth, Middlesex, England

First published by Penguin Books (NZ) Ltd, 2000

3 5 7 9 10 8 6 4 2

Front/back cover photographs: Sunflowers in summer (Allan Parker).
Back cover: Wild poppies in spring (Allan Parker).
Allan and harvest time at San Clemente (Sue Beachman).
A hardware shop in Pienza (Allan Parker).

Editorial services by Michael Gifkins & Associates
Designed by Mary Egan
Typeset by Egan-Reid Ltd, Auckland
Printed in Australia by Australian Print Group, Maryborough

Contents

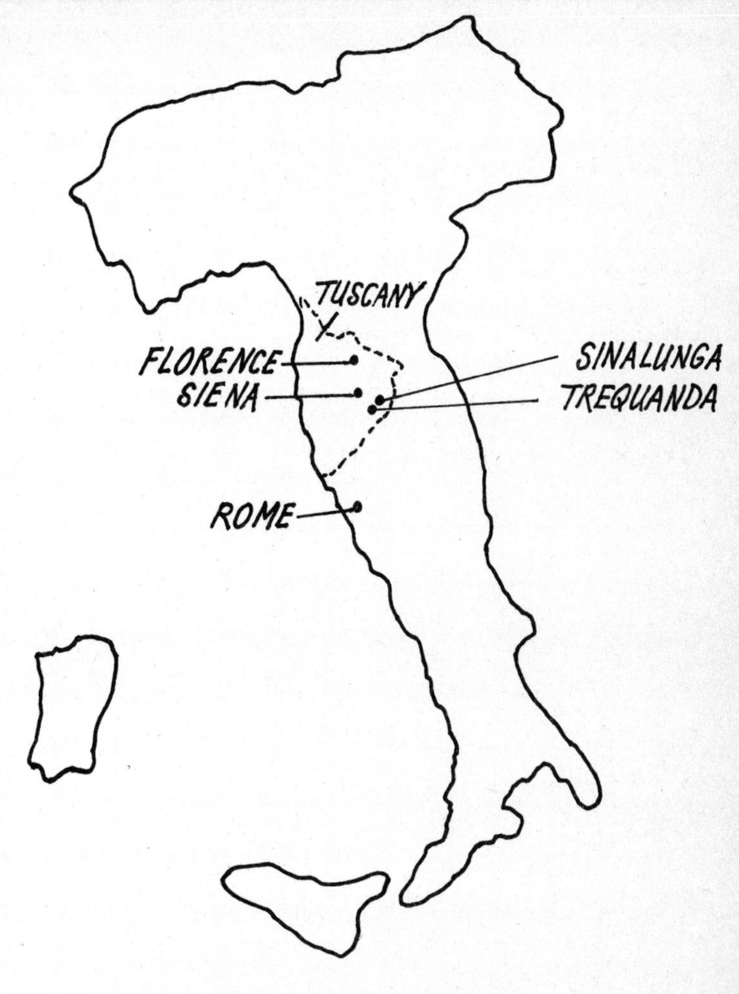

Approximate distances from San Clemente to . . .

Trequanda	**6 kms**
Sinalunga	**15 kms**
Siena	**55 kms**
Florence	**100 kms**
Rome	**180 kms**

CHAPTER ONE

Body Shots in the Farmhouse

IT STARTED IN the warmth of an English summer. I had already seen and experienced many memorable sights and places during a journey through the United States and Canada and arrived in England physically exhausted from my journey, with a vague notion to head for some Greek island and a Mediterranean winter.

One weekend in August, I visited an old school friend in Bedfordshire. He had been house-sitting the holiday villa of an Italian businessman in Tuscany for the last seven years. He and his wife had returned to England in the winter before I arrived, but perhaps he had some contact who might know of similar positions. As it turned out, the villa was empty; the replacement house-sitters had been a disaster. So we rang Carlo, the owner, on the first night of my visit and by Sunday night the position was mine.

It sounded too idyllic to be true. Perhaps it was arrogant to assume I could simply walk into another country where the only language I knew was 'Ciao, baby' and 'Sophia Loren'. I knew little of the history, less of the culture and less still of the customs. It was a daunting and interesting prospect, to say the least.

As it was to be some weeks before I left for Italy, I decided to visit the historic city of Bath. I had passed through it briefly many years before on an earlier expedition to the northern hemisphere. A friend in New Zealand had given me the name of a couple of pubs and their regulars; if I got the chance, could I please say hello to them.

Bath is a delightful city, rich in Roman and English history. I was but the latest visitor in a parade that had been continuing for thousands of years — Celts, Romans, Saxons, Normans, and today's non-stop army of international tourists. The focus of the earlier arrivals was the healing waters of its famous spa, where wealthy Romans lounged and soaked in the great temple and bathing complex that was rediscovered by the Victorians thirteen centuries after dereliction and ruin in the wake of the fall of the Roman Empire. High above the steep hills on which the city rises above the River Avon there is the majestic sweeping arc of John Wood's celebrated Royal Crescent, a Palladian masterpiece. Spanning the Avon is the magnificent Pulteney Bridge, similar to the Ponte Vecchio I was to discover in Florence. I followed in famous footsteps as I walked the streets. The first king of all England, Edgar, was crowned in Bath's beautiful Abbey in 973. The posthumous victor of Trafalgar, Lord Nelson, and Clive of India made homes there, as did the composer Handel. Dickens, Shelley and Sir Walter Scott found inspiration for their writing in Bath.

Ye Olde Farmhouse was a modest little pub high above the city. I had already been there earlier in the week and met some of Dave's rather eccentric friends. As I was leaving Bath on Sunday, I decided to take the steep walk up to the pub to say goodbye to them.

As I went in, a rather interesting looking woman came striding across the road, so I held the door open for her. A brusque and barely audible thanks was my reward. She turned into the alcove on the right; I carried on past the bar and out into the tiny courtyard area on the street where I had first introduced myself to Dave's friends. But they weren't there that night. Back at the bar the woman was sitting talking to Defty, the ex-county off-spinner; I had watched part of an England-Australia cricket test with him at a downtown pub earlier that same day. This recent acquaintanceship provided an ideal opportunity to say hello.

Defty and I spoke briefly about the cricket and then I introduced myself. She said hello and told me her name. 'Are you a musician?' she asked, pointing to the French Quarter T-shirt that I had bought in New Orleans earlier in the year.

'No, I'm having a mid-life crisis,' I responded, quite wittily I thought. Then I told her that I was a New Zealand journalist who had just spent some months travelling through her country (it was obvious from her accent that she was American) and that I was on my way to Tuscany. Just five days before I had heard about San Clemente so was eager to share my good news to anyone with the patience to listen.

'What part of the States are you from?' I asked.

'New Jersey.'

'No one comes from New Jersey. And if they do, they don't admit it,' I said. I had read jokes about the crime, poverty and sheer ugliness of Newark.

She was an intriguing woman, this Nancy May from New Jersey. She drank pints of beer rather than frilly cocktails, she could swear with the best of them, she said 'toilet' or 'loo' rather than 'bathroom', that ridiculous euphemism most of her countryfolk insist on using. She was, she said, on a year's assignment in England to act as a liaison between her American-based pharmaceutical company and its English partner company, developing a new drug.

She had come to the pub — her local — that night to say farewell to one of the bar staff who was leaving for another country. As the evening wore on, the barman and one of his colleagues began drinking shots of tequila.

'That's really rude,' Nancy said. 'If you're doing Mexican poppers you should be offering the customer some. And, anyway, that's not how you should be doing it. You should be doing the Body Shot.'

This naturally aroused everyone's interest, my own included. What was a Body Shot with tequila? It sounded rather risqué. And it was.

With tequila you normally take your shot of liquor, lick the webbing between your thumb and forefinger and sprinkle on some salt and have a slice of lemon at the ready. Lick the salt, drink the shot and suck the lemon.

But the Body Shot requires two people. Lick your partner's neck and sprinkle salt on his/her neck and suck the lemon from his/her mouth.

By now, I had had a few beers so promptly and boldly offered to do one with Nancy. She had had a few, too. So she agreed, with one of those expressions that says, 'I don't believe I'm doing this.'

We lined up a shot for her on the bar, she put the lemon between her lips and I licked and sprinkled her neck. I could see that sucking the lemon would involve a lot of serious lip-to-lip contact and I didn't want to be offensive. So after the shot and the salt-licking I just took the whole lemon slice, skin and all, from her mouth and chewed it up.

Then she had to respond with a Body Shot on me. By now I was feeling somewhat more emboldened. As we sat down I reached out and put my hand on her knee, rather nervously, like a 16-year-old on his first date with a girl. She put her hand on mine. Then she said she had to go! Her mother was staying for a week and she didn't want to leave her too long. The next day they were going to London for some sightseeing.

By this time our hands seemed permanently linked, as they were when we walked to her apartment near The Circus. On her street corner I stopped, took her into my arms and we kissed. The cliché is true, my heart was racing.

I was falling madly and rapidly for this woman called Nancy. The wonder was, she seemed to be feeling the same.

I have to agree that the notion of 'love at first night' does seem a nonsense. I had not been looking for nor did I want a relationship, having recently come from a failed marriage. As two strangers in a foreign land we met one night and I could not take my mind off her. Four days later I wrote to her: 'I think once I'm settled in [I was referring to Tuscany] I'll have to lure you across with some Kiwi version of the New Jersey Body Shot!'

A few days later, back in Bedfordshire, a card came. It was from Nancy. She said she was going to accept my invitation to visit. She added that I'd be welcome to come back to Bath to see her.

'I have a spare bedroom,' she added.

With time on my hands before leaving for Tuscany, I went again to Bath. It was supposed to be for the weekend but it was to last for five days. I displayed my very limited punting skills on the River Avon and we had a champagne picnic in a field by its banks. We listened to the jazz of the John Martin Trio at the Farmhouse. We walked the streets. We dined in and out. And we fell more deeply in love.

I was agonising over what to do. My heart said stay in England with Nancy. My mind said, 'Don't be stupid, Tuscany is too good an opportunity to miss. You've never been to Italy. Do it.' Fortunately Nancy agreed.

Soon I would be leaving. What was to become of our relationship? And what was waiting for me in Tuscany, Trequanda and San Clemente?

CHAPTER TWO

Arrival and Discovery

NANCY WAS LOVE at first night, San Clemente was love at first sight.

If Michelangelo had had the world as his canvas, he might well have created the landscape of San Clemente. My new home stood proud like a mighty granite boulder in the midst of a wide, wide river, disrupting the flow of the land sweeping down around it towards an unseen ocean.

Later I would come to think of it as Adam's outstretched finger reaching out for spiritual grace and intellectual strength from God in his 'Creation of Adam' high atop the Sistine Chapel, fittingly just two hours or so away. The first length of finger is gently sloped. Adam's knuckle is where San Clemente sits on my landscape and then the 'finger' drops steeply to the valley floor below.

From its perch, San Clemente looks smugly down to the flat plain of the Valdichiana and, beyond, the foothills of the Italian spine, the Apennine mountain range.

San Clemente seems ageless and in one way it is, as its age is unknown by its current owner, the former peasant boy who lived there years ago. But Carlo thinks it must be 300 years old, since it was named after one of the early Italian saints. It certainly has a less complicated building style than the other farmhouses that surround me. The building is a simple rectangle in design while the other old houses have the distinctive outside stairway leading up to a colonnaded and arched gallery — an architectural feature much favoured in the time of the *mezzadria*, or sharecropping, era that dominated Tuscany for hundreds of years.

To reach San Clemente, I drive from my local village, Trequanda, towards the equally small town of Montisi. Perhaps 700 metres outside Trequanda I turn left onto the road to Petroio, the justifiably self-proclaimed 'terracotta capital of the world'. This winding country road — alarmingly narrow when I encounter large trucks carting roof tiles or quarried stone — runs across the face of the valley slope.

The two highest peaks (599 and 642 metres above sea level) are known as Piazze di Siena, presumably because you can see that famed city from their tops. From San Clemente, the skyline of this ridge of hills looks like a woman's torso and upper legs as she lies on her stomach. To the right is her rising shoulders and back, tapering to her waist where the first peak falls away. The next, lower, peak is her bottom. The third peak is softer, lower still and gentler. This is the back of her thigh. The locals call these hills *i monti*. I call them 'My Lady of the Mountains'.

Realistically, they are more high hills than mountains but this is how they have been named. To my left, the hill falls away to farmland and on down to the valley below. Isolated farmhouses lie scattered across it like toasted croutons on the surface of a rich Tuscan *pappa al pomodori* broth.

After some kilometres, I come to the turning to the one-vehicle, unpaved lane that winds down to San Clemente, through the farm fields that encircle me on three sides. It is a difficult entrance to find for first-time visitors — a narrow cut in the trees and sudden dip down, so the lane's surface is obscured from the Petroio road.

Sometimes, driving down to the villa, I am mindful of my place in the scheme of things. Ten centuries ago, Etruscans built this road — the paving stones of their ancient civilisation are still in place in one section of the road beyond San Clemente as it drops down to its exit near Sinalunga. A half-kilometre further on from the villa, where the old monastery I know as Miciano now stands, Roman centurions stationed themselves; it is a place that commands a powerful view over the valley below. Perhaps they used mirrored glass and the sun to flash warnings of invasion from the north to colleagues stationed high in the hillside town of Cortona on the opposite side of the valley, itself one of the most important locations in Etruscan history?

This strategic value was recognised by other warriors in more modern times. German artillery units and observation posts were stationed in the hills here during the last world war.

Travellers throughout history have walked, ridden or driven along this now-meagre thoroughfare. It has been an important transport artery for centuries, linking Rome, Siena and Florence. Along its winding route have come pilgrims, monks, soldiers, Knights of the Templar Cross, farmers leading their ox-drawn carts and produce to market, nobility on their way to the Medici courts of Florence or the papal glory of St Peter's Basilica in Rome . . . the rich, the famed, the powerful and the commonplace. Today these travellers prefer the unrutted convenience of the autostrada and the lane has fallen into unused disrepair. Modern travellers still pass by — hunters, tourists on foot, farm workers, cycle and trailbike riders, and vacationing owners of the apartments that have been created at the old monastery of Miciano.

But these modern wayfarers lack the romance and history of those ages past. Who will remember them in some distant future compared to the personalities that once walked this way? The 'pitiless scoundrel' Ghino di Tacco, an 11th century highwayman, kidnapper and plunderer. When one of his brothers and an uncle were condemned to death, he rode to Rome, beheaded their judge and returned to his castle with the head impaled on a lance. There he displayed his trophy from the highest tower. Later he was to become a papal knight to Pope Bonifacio VIII. He died in an ambush near Sinalunga and his memory was captured by both Dante, in the 6th cantide of the *Purgatorio*, and Boccaccio, who dedicated the second novella of the tenth day to him in the *Decameron*.

And what 20th century trailbiker will be remembered ahead of Bartolomeo Garosi, who was to become known as Il Brandano and 'God's madman'? He was born in Petroio in 1486 and grew into a sinful life of drinking, gambling and blasphemy until a 'revelation' turned him to God. The 'revelation' was actually a stone chip that struck him in the head and eye when he was digging one day. Alarmed by this heavenly sign, he was converted one Good Friday, mock-crucified in the manner of the robber next to Jesus at Calvary. History records that 'he mocked the winter barefoot and wearing only a Hessian sack' as part of his penance when he was raised on the Cross. Leaving his family, he embarked on a solo preaching campaign throughout Italy and other European countries, crucifix in one hand and, for some unrecorded reason, a skull in the other. On a later occasion he turned up in Rome distributing *ossi di morti* (bones of the dead) to no doubt alarmed prelates and even Pope Clement VII himself. The disgruntled Pope had him chained in a sack and thrown into a river. But like some 16th century

Houdini he triumphantly emerged from the water, announcing the imminent fall of Rome and the death of the Pope who had had the audacity to treat him so callously!

These characters are the stuff of history, not some modern cyclist clad in designer gear.

And so I have come home. One last steep dip in the lane and I am at the base of Michelangelo's knuckle. From here I look up and across a field to San Clemente's bulk, fully 500 square metres of peasant farmhouse. From here it is just a short drive along the lane to the house.

My first view of the villa was masked by night — a 3 am arrival after a nightmarish seventeen-hour journey from England. Later I was to register the four double bedrooms upstairs, each with its own en suite shower, all built round a large central area with huge fireplace and library of books in English, Italian, German and French. The entrance way was as big as an average apartment and there was a grand piano in the lounge, protecting a wall covered with hundreds of record albums. In the farmhouse-style kitchen was a six-burner hob stove.

Later, my rose-tinted glasses would become more realistically coloured with the mud of autumn and the dust of spring and summer. I would back my freezing body against the central heating radiators as icy winds sneaked into the house through cracks in the panels of the doors. For three days the first winter I lived in the kitchen when the central heating failed, keeping warm — by closing the doors and running the oven and gas hobs. The two magnificent fireplaces were no source of solace or warmth. Their hoods were too high so more smoke came into the room than went up the chimney.

If San Clemente was my home, Trequanda was my social centre. The small village is typical of so many of the hilltop medieval towns and hamlets, perched on a ridge some 462 metres above sea level. It is about five kilometres from the villa, hidden from me by the spurs and ridges running down from *i monti*.

Trequanda is not a place of great riches. It does not have the historical treasures of Etruscan Chiusi. It does not command the same sweeping panoramas as Cortona, nor possess the architectural beauty of papal-blessed Pienza. It does not have a mighty castle like Montalcino. It has no great domed church like Montepulciano's San Baggio. It is not blessed with the hot thermal spa waters of so many of the surrounding towns . . . Chianciano Terme, Bagno Vignoni, Bagno San Filippo.

But like a farmyard hen pecking for wheat, it has picked up enough grains to provide a filling feast for the new invaders coming from the north, the ever-increasing numbers of tourists from Germany, Switzerland, Holland, France, Belgium, Austria, England and even far-away America.

It does have a view to Siena. In its steeply falling arched alleyways it has a certain architectural beauty. It does have an Etruscan history. And it does have a castle.

In its own modest way, then, Trequanda has picked up enough of Tuscan history and culture to give it a charm of its own.

It is the administrative centre of the commune of Trequanda that covers nearly 70 square kilometres, more than a third still forested. The district also incorporates the towns of Petroio and Castelmuzio. About 1500 people live within its boundary, with Trequanda the main population centre.

The town's name remains an enigma. Local books suggest it could have sprung from a variety of sources. Perhaps it comes from the Tarkonte, a legendary hero of the days when Etruscans settled here. Or perhaps the name derives from *terram quandam*, a special or isolated place, or from a *tregua* or truce perhaps signed here, or from *tre-guarda*, from its three entrance gates. The town's coat of arms — three silver chalices on a red background — could be another source — from a regional dialect where chalice or cup is *quanda*. The true origins of the name will never be known — a fire centuries ago in the archives of Arezzo destroyed pre-1200 records of the village.

Throughout the centuries, however, it has been of strategic interest to the warring states and nations which have passed this way, its location on a range of hills separating the important Val d'Asso and Valdichiana valleys. Millions of years ago, the waters of the Mediterranean covered the valley floors below these hills. Later, it was an important centre on the travel routes between Chiusi and Siena through the Sienese 'badlands', Le Crete.

In the first centuries of the current millennium, the village was the residence of branches of the Cacciaconti family who owned vast landholdings in the area. Evidence of their presence remains in the imposing castle that occupies fully one third of the old, oval-shaped village that rises, cone-like, above the former town walls. The castle provides Trequanda with its most distinctive feature, a squat circular tower uncommon in these parts. A cypress tree grows through the brickwork of the castle walls, which still retain their turret battlements.

The gate to the castle opens on to the town's focal point, the Piazza Garibaldi. Barely 70 metres long and 20 metres wide, it is lined by the more important civic, religious and social institutions. If I stand at its entrance, looking down its gently sloped rectangle, I will have the small church of the Immacolata (Chiesa Compagnia) on my right. This is part of the castle complex but adopts a different role on summer evenings when the old men of the village sit on its steps to watch, literally, the world go by as tourists gather for pre-dinner drinks.

In the right-hand corner of the square is the entrance to the main road running into the town, a steep rise that passes the castle walls and is aptly named Via Cacciaconti. The narrow opening was once able to be sealed by a huge wooden door, one of three such entranceways into the otherwise walled village.

Down the right-hand long side of the *piazza* one finds the small branch of one of Italy's many banks. In the 'season', I was told, I would need to go early for changing money before the tourists drained it of ready cash. Next door is the pharmacy, with the emerald green neon cross that denotes all pharmacies in Italy. Next to that is the town hall with its high, square, thin and turreted tower with a clock dating from 1380. It no longer works. Perhaps it hasn't worked for the last 600 years? Beneath it is the office of the town constable, with the Post Office next door again.

The piazza then leaps across a street entrance to its parish church dedicated to Saint Peter and Saint Andrew. The first stone of its gothic-romanesque façade was laid in 1327. Among its minor art treasures is a fresco of the Ascension by the famed Renaissance artist Giovanni Antonio Bazzi, or Sodoma. A highly decorated wooden urn contains the remains of Beata Bonizzella Cacciaconti, a noblewoman of the family who ruled the land in medieval times. Becoming widowed, she retired to one of the large farm estate properties that surround Trequanda (Belsedere, today one of Tuscany's ubiquitous *agroturismo* centres for tourists) to devote her life to charity. After her death, her memory died too, until years later her burial site was discovered. Her body, tradition has it, was in a state that suggested she had died just hours before the discovery. Beside it were the remains of a child, thought to be her grandchild. Local legend tells that when her body was taken to the church where she now rests, a Spanish soldier from one of the many invading armies that have marched through this beautiful but often-bloodied land, took a ring from her finger. He immediately went blind, his sight restored only when he returned the ring. She has also been hailed as a saviour of the town's women from the potential ravages of raiding soldiers. Each May, her life and after-life feats are celebrated by the town. But for the rest of the year, it is the Catholic Mass that is celebrated, the church bells calling the faithful. On Sundays, the worshippers gather in the square, dressed in their Sunday best, to socialise with friends before the service.

The building along the bottom of the piazza houses apartments, blooming bright red with geraniums in the warm months, and the surgery of the town's *dottore* or doctor.

Coming back up the left side are apartments, a cabinet-maker, the showroom of a local artist, the general goods emporium and the Bar La Siesta, the town's social centre. In summer, holidaymakers sit at its outside tables, reading their English or German newspapers. In winter, the locals return to use it as a base for friendship and company. Travellers from Rome or Florence park their BMWs outside while they have an espresso to relieve the stress of driving. Young children play on its video games. Farmhands from the surrounding country come for a lunchtime beer. The old men sit reading its free newspapers to keep abreast of the world outside, or just to pass another idle day. You can buy a snack, a condom, a postcard or a gelato. It is the only licensed tobacco shop in town. The bus to Sinalunga, Montisi and Petroio stops outside its glassed doors. So, too, does the bright yellow school bus. The neighbouring shopkeepers close their doors throughout the day to visit for a quick coffee. On summer evenings, it spills out to occupy half the piazza with tables and chairs while a singer and musician play live music from a small stage along the opposite wall. These nights of the 'Piano Bar' are an opportunity for its prices to be jacked up, perhaps to cover the cost of the musicians and the rental of the extra furniture. The self-important and wealthier locals and tourists seem happy to pay the extra for the privilege of being seen. Others mill about in the bottom half of the piazza or line the steps of the castle, taking advantage of the free show. In winter it is a smoky haven of warmth and chatter.

In summer the piazza is a bustling place. Delivery trucks and courier vans come and go, shoppers cross with bags of groceries, the cabinetmaker's tools whine, old women stop to gossip, old men sit and gaze, the foreign tongues of tourists mingle with the native tongue of the locals . . .

In winter, though, it is a bleak and barren stretch of openness. The winds sweep across it. Rain, frost and snow make it a cold and bitter place, where people out on business or shopping scurry across it quickly. In this, Trequanda is no different from the other hilltop towns exposed to the whim of the winter elements.

From the piazza, the narrow streets of the town fall sharply to its old walls. Here, in a place of cobblestones and arches, are other shops and businesses among the apartments of the residents. I go down one lane to get my groceries from the local co-op. Further down is a small butcher, another grocery store and a woodworker's workshop. At the end is another of the three old gateways into the town. Down the next street is the bakery. The town's tourist office is in another. Behind Bar La Siesta is Trequanda's sole restaurant, Il Conte Matto, with its menu of local foods and panoramic view towards Siena. Another small street houses the town's hairdresser. The aroma of some delicious lunch being prepared drifts out from the kitchen of one of its houses. Behind the town hall is a small park with a lovely little fountain, tall trees and an area for young children to frolic.

Beyond the boundaries of the old walls, Trequanda's 'new town' is expanding. On my way back to San Clemente, I pass the garage where I get my petrol with the carabiniere station next door. Opposite the garage is the Passe-Partout hardware store. Here I can buy anything from drainage pipe to flypaper to crockery. Turning out of the town, onto the road to Montisi, Petroio and San Clemente, I pass the Macelleria Ricci, my butcher's shop, the Bar Paradiso bar and gelateria (a favoured haunt of the local teen set) and the veterinary clinic where I take San Clemente's resident canine, Molly, for examinations and toe-nail clipping. Elegant new houses line the high ridge on the left. Hidden behind this lies the local soccer field; on winter Sundays, the cheering and clapping of the spectators reaches across the fields to San Clemente. Here, too, is the tower of the Molino a Vento, a 300-year-old dovecote with more than 600 nests in its walls, reached by a spiral staircase.

Ugly square apartment blocks rise from the ground as the ridge falls away on the right. Below me is the town's swimming pool (amazingly, only open for two or so months at the very peak of the summer heat) and tennis court complex, laid out with surrounding lawn and bar/café. It is a popular place on hot days but expensive, as many of the pools and spas of this region appear to be.

So this was to be my home. It was a very different world from the one I had left behind in New Zealand or passed through on my travels before arriving at San Clemente's glass-panelled doorway. Here I would have to move into survival mode — to learn the language, the culture, the rules of a new land. I would have to acquaint myself with such basics as using the telephone, what food to get, how to find my way around, what road signs were telling me to do (or not to do), where to buy dog food, how to get central heating oil delivered . . . and all in a totally unknown language.

I had to learn how to communicate. I needed to know the words for food and other essentials — tomatoes (*pomodori*), bread (*pane*), butter (*burro*), mushrooms (*funghi*), milk (*latte*), fill-it-up (*pieno*). More complex matters would be particularly trying and nerve-wracking — 'the television isn't working', 'when can you come?', 'I need a new gas bottle'. My ignorance of Italian was not helped by my limited understanding of French. The languages are very similar in spelling but totally different in pronunciation — French is a softer, silkier tongue with many vowels and consonants unstated, whereas Italians pronounce everything.

My isolation at San Clemente did not help. I had limited contact with the outside world. My nearest neighbour spoke English and I could select my food by hand from shop shelves or from market stalls by pointing. The need for Italian conversation on these occasions was limited. At other times, mime and gesture would be enough to get by.

The telephone, however, became a thing to dread. To order, say, fuel oil meant preparing a written question(s) from the dictionary or language book that were never far from my reach. Without any knowledge of tenses, I would have to try to use these in the present tense to get my message across. This, naturally, required a response from the other party, the point at which the real problems began.

Italians seem genetically incapable of talking at less than 400 words a minute. Time after time, I would hopefully but helplessly ask, 'Piano, piano, per favore' ('Slowly, slowly, please'). In France, many years before, 'Lentement, s'il vous plaît' had become my most-used phrase as I tried to understand a rapid-fire sentence with my schoolboy French.

Here in Italy such requests did not fall on deaf ears; the people nodded their understanding — but would simply carry on at a mile-a-minute pace. I am sure they knew my problem and were trying to help. They were just not capable of speaking slowly for a hapless foreigner. To be fair, that was, ultimately, my problem; I had chosen to come here and it should be up to me to adapt to the conditions of my host country. But with no knowledge of the language this was a daunting task.

From my first arrival, I was urged: 'You must learn Italian. Take the course at Siena University [it has a famous school for foreigners to learn the Italian language and culture].' This was a fine suggestion in principle but practical matters proscribed it. First there was the economic cost — and without an income I had to guard my money. Then there was the time and travel — the course was three hours a day, Monday to Friday, for three months — a round trip of nearly 100 kilometres each day. And as I knew Nancy was coming to visit, I did not want such a commitment to interfere with the precious little time we would have together.

So I struggled on with my limp attempts to cope with this new language. My ability to read the language improved; so many words have a close similarity to either English or French. But conversational Italian I found hard to follow because of its speed. Italian television was not only fast but numbingly banal. I even bought an Italian language course set of cassette tapes on one trip to New Jersey and, yes, it was just as fast and just as useless.

It was to be a year before we met Joe, the English-speaking German from Petroio who had been living in Italy for many years. He agreed to give Nancy and myself weekly lessons and so we began visiting his small apartment in the next village, sitting around the table in the cramped kitchen with dog at our feet and cat on Nancy's lap as we went back to school in Italy. Nouns, verb conjugations, definite articles, indefinite articles . . . grammar lessons I thought I had long left behind me.

Even so, I knew it would be a task of years. One expatriate who had lived here for fourteen years and spoke, to my ears, fluent Italian said even she never expected to master it. The language is flowery and emotional with subtle nuances. This much I could pick up from the style in the national newspapers like *La Nazione.*

But if learning fluent Italian was to be a project of years, survival in Trequanda was to be my primary mission.

CHAPTER THREE

A New World in the Old

THE CITIES, TOWNS and villages that surround San Clemente are as gloriously rich as the countryside. Some — Florence, Siena, Cortona — are redolent with history. Others — Pianocastagnaio, Lucignano, Montepulciano — border on the unpronounceable. Yet others — Sinalunga, Scrofiano, Montefollonico — sound like nasty social diseases.

Within an hour, I can view a pre-Christian Etruscan tomb, admire Michelangelo's David, plunge into a steaming mineral pool or walk a battlefield where Hannibal defeated the Romans. I can see the world's finest olive oil being pressed, admire the magnificence of Siena's Duomo, stroll the street where Dante was born or admire the views from the church where St Francis of Assisi lies buried or the prehistoric cave where he prayed. I can see a 40,000-year-old site of human settlement — one of central Italy's oldest — or pretend I am a Roman consul in a hot thermal spa.

My new world, I soon discovered, is one to revel in; I felt at the centre of a very special universe. From my hillside eyrie I look over the flat plain of the Valdichiana with the spine of Italy, the Apennines, providing a theatrical backdrop. The valley is one of the most extensive in the mountain chain, some 500 square kilometres of flat land that over the centuries has been drowned marshland, drained farmland, drowned again and reclaimed. Roman legions once marched its length. Barbarians and Vandals plundered it on their rampage to destroy Rome, and Carthaginian soldiers fed themselves and their warhorses from its cereal farms.

But even before that it was populated by that mysterious race, the Etruscans, who roamed these hills, valleys and plains thousands of years ago. Today, evidence of their presence can be seen in tombs, museums and ruins that are all that now remains of their ancient civilisation. Large towns nearby — Arezzo, Chiusi and Cortona are examples — were all autonomous kingdoms that formed part of a twelve-city marriage of Etruscan convenience. At night, the lights of Cortona wink at me directly across the Valdichiana, high up a steep mountain ridge. Its alleyways and roads are, like so many of the hill towns of Tuscany, narrow, cobbled, dark and beautiful.

This is the region that has been a crossroads of history through the ages. Through here runs the Via Cassia created by the Romans after their triumphant march north to conquer the Etruscans. The modern equivalent is the autostrada, or A1, the main motorway linking Rome with the great cities of the north — Florence, Milan, Bologna. It slashes through the Valdichiana, its chariots now bearing names like Fiat and Mercedes.

And in the valley behind, Val d'Asso, beyond the ridge of *i monti*, another famous road was to develop as Europe woke into the Medieval Age. The Via Francigena, or Franciscan Way, became the main artery between Rome and the northern plains. It provided the major trade link between the North Sea and the

Mediterranean and supported a network of fortress towns, abbeys, monasteries and havens for weary travellers. It passed by towns that were to become very familiar to me — Montalcino, Buonconvento, San Quirico d'Orcia, Torrienieri . . .

Knights Templar of the Crusades maintained a garrison network to provide shelter and support for travellers. From the door of San Clemente I can see the skyline silhouette of Abbadia Sicile, founded by the Knights nearly eight centuries ago as such a resting place and still bearing two sculpted crosses of the Order. Another cross is at the entrance to my neighbourhood village, Petroio.

My nearest 'big town' is Sinalunga, about 15 kilometres from San Clemente by road but only seven or eight in a straight line. From the far end of the back garden, I can see it spilling down the hilltop to the valley floor. Its skyline is dominated by the distinctive bell tower of the old church of San Martino, its cupola sprouting weeds and grass blown from the fields below. The church remains the focal point of the ancient walled village. With two other churches as well as the town hall, two bars and a variety of traders, it fronts onto the cobbled Piazza Garibaldi, the main square. The only notable feature of the square is that it is possible to drive through it, like Trequanda's Piazza Garibaldi. Most towns have sealed off their centres to private vehicles. Most have also named a piazza after Garibaldi, that great figure in Italian history. At least Sinalunga can claim some right to his name — he was arrested there in 1867 by the royal carabinieri while embarked on another campaign to liberate Rome.

Like Flaubert's village of Clochemerle, Sinalunga has its own human waste scandal. You can smell its foul odour each time you pass along the climbing road between the town and Trequanda. Rubbish is collected daily by private contractors and delivered to the town dump. For some reason, it creates the most obnoxious smell — so thick each time you pass through it that you feel you could cut out a piece of the atmosphere to take home and cultivate. The problem became a major *cause célèbre* amongst the local population, with petitions, an 'anti-dump' organisation, proposals to relocate it, calls to sack the contractors . . . but still the problem persisted throughout my first year. As I drove new visitors past it on the way to San Clemente I would quickly assure them that no one had let rip with a surreptitious fart. Some brave-hearted — or foolhardy — soul bought an abandoned farmhouse across the road and spent many, many thousands of dollars restoring it, even though the problem of this rubbish dump from hell remained unresolved.

Like most towns in my vicinity, Sinalunga was built on a hilltop not so much to admire the views but as defensive protection against the armies that have marched through here over the centuries. During the great 15th century struggle for control of the land between Siena and the Medici stronghold of Florence, most held allegiance to one or other of the warring camps and thus faced attack or siege. All these towns — Montefollonico, Montepulciano, Cortona, Montalcino — stand on the hills that make these areas visually attractive. Their spires, towers and turrets form pointed silhouettes against the skyline as they tumble down the hillsides from the old town centres at the top. In the rising or setting sun, their brown brick buildings and tiled rooftops glow a burnished copper in the light. At night, the more important buildings of each town are flood-lit — evocative, silent sentinels that seem almost ethereal against the backdrop of the night sky. Even out on the valley floor, there were a few small hills on which to build a fortress town. From San Clemente I can see Lucignano, Foiano, Bettolle . . .

One day in early April, I sought fame and fortune on the Yellow

Brick Road. Hollywood had been in town for a week at Montepulciano. The town's main piazza was set up as a market place for a new Hollywood 'take' on Shakespeare's *Midsummer Night's Dream*. The stars were Michelle Pfieffer, Kevin Kline and Danny Devito. The choice of a Tuscan town was not surprising. The beautiful town of Pienza, a dozen or so kilometres from Montepulciano, was the setting for Zeffirelli's *Romeo and Juliet*. And even Trequanda has had its moment of big-screen glory as the setting for a Peter Ustinov film in the early post-war years. A nearby abbey was used as a set for *The English Patient*. This part of Tuscany is like that. I wanted to catch a bit of the action, find out more about the movie and, secretly, hoped I'd be 'discovered' and begged to join the local townsfolk who had been hired as extras. I would track down the PR person, talk a bit about the movie and then casually throw in: 'What chance of being an extra?' It all seemed very straightforward. After all, some 350 of the local townsfolk had already been hired as extras. Why not one more?

Saying 'ciao' to Molly, the gentle, loving, ageing German Shepherd who 'came' with the house, I left San Clemente armed with camera, notebook, newspaper clippings of the 'event' and a pocketful of dreams. At the top of my road I turned left and south towards Montepulciano, the still bare woods of *i monti* on my right and the flat open expanse of the Valdichiana away below me. I passed the tiny farm estate of Abbadia Sicile, a monastery built by the Knights Templar 700 years ago as a medieval motel. If I turned left here, I would drive down past the abbey and the seafood restaurant, Le Logge, to the outskirts of Sinalunga.

But my route took me right, past the ugly banality of a large stone quarry then through woods where huge piles of felled limbs were stacked for the next winter. Who owns the woods, I wondered. Who has the rights to fell the trees? In the thinned copses, smaller stacks were neatly piled. I passed olive groves and vineyards, the vines pruned bare awaiting the coming budding of the grapes. The fields were a mosaic of colour — emerald green where ploughed soil was bearing new growth, russet ploughed soil merged into mud-grey soil like the mud that spews to the surface in the thermal heartland of New Zealand. Signposts pointed to the place names that have become familiar friends I know will live on with me forever — Castelmuzio, Montisi, Montefollonico, San Quirico d'Orcia, Torrita di Siena, Pienza. It was an imposing panorama as I crested ridges and dropped down hillsides.

My route also took me past local farm shops selling the famous products of the land here — olive oil, pecorino and ricotta cheese, *cinghiale* or wild boar salami, *miele* (honey) in all its different-flavoured glory and, of course, *vino nobile*. For I am not in the land of Chianti to the north or Montalcino's Brunello of the west. No, this is the region of the 'King of Wines', Montepulciano's ancient juice of the vine, with other Tuscan wines among the world's best.

Even as I walked into Montepulciano I passed the Cantina Gottavecchi, nestled, somehow fittingly, with the buildings and grounds of the Chiesa de Santa Maria dei Servi. The cellars proudly proclaim: 'Grotte del 1200'.

And so up the street beneath the soaring stones of the old town walls. The signs of Hollywood quickly became evident — large equipment trunks with entrails of thick cables spilling up the narrowing old town streets towards the central Piazza Grande with its 13th century Palazzo and bland Duomo.

My interest quickened as I approached the piazza. Was this to be the big chance?

Well, no. The only sign of animated life was a group of tourists being lectured by a guide in the centre of the square. Perhaps, I thought, Sunday is a day of rest. But having read about the exorbitant cost of a full film crew each day, I suspected not. I asked a signora in one of the piazza's shops if the filming was finished for the day to, perhaps, be back on again *domani*. 'Finito a Piazza,' she told me — the location filming fuss had ended the day before and the film had been transferred to Rome for studio shooting.

And so my quest was over before it began. I consoled myself by buying a copy of *La Nazione* as I made my way back to the car and to San Clemente. My journey was a farcical non-event and I remain, as ever, unrenowned and fortuneless. I should have realised how futile the effort was to be as I began this quest. The Yellow Brick Road was, rather, my dusty, rocky, steep and narrow lane up the hill from San Clemente.

As populations and urbanisation have increased in these towns, 'suburbs' have sprung up below the old walls. Some, like Sinalunga, now spill out onto the plain of the valley floor below, housing new homes, shopping centres, schools, railway stations . . . but as you walk through the narrow cobbled alleys, made dim by the dense three-storied old buildings that hem them in so closely, it is possible to drift back to the life they contained as long as a millennium ago. You can imagine the clatter of hoof and cartwheel, the pounding of the blacksmith's hammers, the strutting of the nobles, the shouting of the vendors, the drifting smoke from the chestnut brazier . . . a romantic image that ignores the stink of the horse and human droppings, the encrusted grime from the open fires and the squalor of the poor.

But in such a land of romance, I prefer to hold the gentler picture in my mind.

A side product of this reach-for-the-stars hilltop development of the old towns is the stamina the residents need to climb their steep and snaking streets. It is a source of constant wonder how the people cope with them, particularly the old folk. Black-garbed, bow-legged old ladies stoically trudge back up to their homes, a heavy grocery bag in each hand. Bent old men with canes strolling up to the market for companionship and coffee. At times, they seem a super-race. Is it some genetic or dietary factor that bows their legs so? Or the weight of Catholic guilt they have to carry on their shoulders? It seems as good a reason as any.

While the towns appear much the same as one another, they can lay claim to different features. It may be the spectacular view over vineyards and olive groves from Montepulciano's old walls. It may be the Etruscan tombs of Chiusi. It may be Montalcino's imposing castle.

These distinctions aside, they each share more than a strategic location. Their churches are filled with rich religious paintings and their populations take great pride in the history, culture and architecture that surrounds them. The towns are kept meticulously clean and, in summer, householders festoon their outside walls and street fronts with window boxes and planters that blaze with flowers. How unlike the graffitied walls and littered streets of my homeland!

Of all these towns, my favourite was to be Pienza. Nancy and I were to discover it together and, as we sat in warm autumn sun on its wall, decide that it was 'our town'.

It was created by Rossellino on instructions from Pope Pius II, who wanted his birthplace to become the perfect Renaissance town, fusing the elements that were distinctly part of that great 15th century era of architecture, learning, art and civility.

Today, it is recognised as one of the gems in the Renaissance crown, even though the full project died along with the Pope — just two years after it began. As no one else emerged to show interest in, let alone pay for, completing the vision, all that remains today are the main buildings facing the small central

Piazza Pio II — the cathedral, and Pope Pius's and other palaces. But beyond these imposing buildings has arisen a small town of around 2500 people, possessed of great character and charm. Its tiny, narrow streets and alleys are a constant visual treat and, in summer, come alive with potted blooms.

It has become very much a tourist mecca and its streets in summer are a meandering mass of sightseers. But it still manages to retain its elegance and beauty in the face of this invasion. The people created these towns to provide physical shelter. But they also created structures for their spiritual character. This is a land that has long sought solace from gods — the Etruscans, the Romans and in more modern times, the Catholic Church. One needs little reminding that less than two hours from San Clemente sits the centre of this powerful religion, a papal state within a state.

There is Sant'Antimo, its vaulted austerity filled with the Gregorian chants of its current custodians. But none, surely throughout all Italy, can match the beauty of Monte Oliveto Maggiore. By any reckoning, it is a majestic building in an even more majestic setting high on a ridge spur deep in the Tuscan country, but a bare 30 minutes from San Clemente. The abbey's russet brickwork with its pointed belltower reaching for the clouds pokes through magnificent cypress firs. In winter, it takes on an almost mystical air as snow frosts the ground and the cypress branches, and mist moves sluggishly around them. Its grounds hold smaller churches, chapels, cloisters and tombs. But for most visitors, the focal point is the cycle of 36 frescoes on the walls of the main building, depicting scenes from the stories of San Benedetto da Norcia as told by St Gregory. The cycle took a decade to complete — from 1497 to 1508, although the abbey's origins date back to 1313 when 'White Benedictine' hermits seeking the austerity of their earliest brethren came to live in hillside caves. These hermits were early founders of the

Olivetan Order. As imposing — even more so to my mind — as the frescoes are the 500-year-old choir stalls, inlaid with intricate, remarkable scenes created by wood panelling.

My northern 'border' is dominated by one of the great cities of Europe, Siena. 'Siena opens up its heart to you more than any other,' proclaims the text on one of the gates to the city. And this was certainly true for Nancy and me. If Pienza was to be our town then Siena was to become our city (although it was a close contest with Florence). From the first walk down the steps from Via di Citta and into the sun-soaked breathtaking expanse of Il Campo, I was captivated. Then there was the equally stunning first sight of the glorious front of the Duomo and the richness of its interior, far more beautiful than the almost bland interior of its more famous Florentine counterpart. On clear days, the distinctive tower of Il Campo's Palazzo Pubblico tower and the great belltower of the Duomo can be seen from Trequanda. Driving towards it, the imposing body of the cathedral, high atop its ridge-line peak, looms closer into view, along with the tumbling houses that line its steeply falling streets. At night, the towers are lit up by spotlights — a beautiful scene for miles around.

Siena, home to Etruscans and Romans, came into its own as a medieval city when it defeated rival Florence in 1260 and emerged as one of the Continent's most powerful centres. A century later, 75 per cent of its citizens were to die as the Black Death ravaged Europe.

Today, the guidebooks will tell you about the artworks, the Palio, the museums and the fortress, Forte di Santa Barbara, which is said to house a bottle of every Italian wine produced. For me, the secret of Siena is its atmosphere — the bizarre nights in the smoke-filled Irish Pub listening to an Italian band playing Irish music, the beautiful simplicity and elegance of its shop window displays (better by far than chic Florence), the pleasure of watching the world go by at an outside café table in Il Campo and the sight of tiled roofs spilling down its alleyways and side streets. Siena is where you can go to find a local bar favoured by the large university student population. There you can order a cheap sandwich from a range of prosciutto, cheese, tomatoes, and antipasti (eggplants, mushrooms, onions) steeped in olive oil.

Tuscany is an intricate system of river-carved valleys separated by hills and mountains. North of Siena, on the route to Florence, the Chianti area is a much steeper terrain, studded with carefully groomed vineyards that produce its famed wine. Sandwiched between these two great centres, it was the first to attract city wealth and, in the modern era, foreign money for holiday villas. But the money was slower to flow into the southern, Sienese, Tuscany that surrounds me. Where farming has developed over the centuries, the land is tended and preened with the love that a farming life breeds. But it also has large tracts of wooded areas where game birds and animals flourish. There is a still-wild air about it. The difference between the Tuscany of Chianti and my Tuscany reminds me of two pageboys at a wedding. Both have been immaculately dressed and scrubbed, their hair slicked down to keep it in place. The Chianti pageboy remains untouched but someone has walked past mine and tousled his hair so that it is slightly messed. His handsome looks are still there but he now has an urchin look about him.

This area is also one of contrasts. The hills immediately about me are soft and curvaceous, rolling seductively across the fields and woods. They are as if some giant sculptor has lovingly smoothed his hands across the landscape, creating gentle, rolling rises and falls across the hillside. To the south and west, the land is more rugged, steep and high. The hills plunge to the river floor rather than flow. There are great rocky outcrops that poke through the forests that clothe them. It is a more abandoned environment.

But the overriding natural feature of the land here is to the north-west — the land of Le Crete, a vast arena of barren clay hills, furrowed in places by erosion but mostly by the plough. For miles these bare rolling hills stretch away, the landscape relieved only by solitary farmhouses and cypress trees scattered along the hilltops.

It is a hushed and lonely world, one that draws you into it with a beauty that intrigues, beguiles and, at times, fills you with a fear of the unknown. Its isolated, eerie atmosphere reminds you of the better known badlands of the old American West.

In autumn, great boulders of sun-baked clay are thrown up by the ploughing discs. In spring and summer an ocean of sunflowers and wheat ripple in the wind. Under the full moon, the grey of the clay turns white in the night, and transforms Le Crete into a mysterious, mystical place.

To the east and south, in the flatland of the Valdichiana, lies my 'Lake District', stretches of inland water that are reminders of the centuries when the valley below me was marshland. The lakes of Montepulciano and Chiusi are important protected natural habitats for birds, fish and plant life. A third, Lake Trasimeno, became a popular visit for us, lying close to Cortona and with added dimensions of history and art. It is actually not in Tuscany; its western edge marks the border of the region of Umbria.

Trasimeno is a shallow lake — only six metres deep at most — but it is Italy's fourth largest, covering 128 square kilometres of Umbrian territory. It has three small islands — Maggiore, Minore and Polvese — accessible by ferry.

On its north-western rim is the popular resort area of Tuoro sul Trasimeno. On an April morning twelve centuries ago, between the town of Tuoro and the lake shore below, the Carthaginian invader Hannibal routed a Roman army. Of the 25,000 Roman soldiers caught in the ambush, 15,000 were slaughtered, including their leader Consul Caius Flaminius Nepote.

Consul Flaminius's army had marched north to stop the rampaging Hannibal from his relentless and ruthless march to Rome. The previous year, Hannibal had set out on his famous expedition from Spain, crossing the Pyrenees and Alps with 50,000 men, 9000 horses and 37 elephants. Most of the elephants died in the cold of the mountains. On his way, northern and Gaelic tribes joined him for his march into the Roman heartland. By the time of the battle at Lake Trasimeno, all the elephants and many of his men had surrendered to epidemics in the marshy land of the Valdichiana. But his army — at 40,000 men — still retained superiority of numbers and weapons as Flaminius pursued him.

On the night before the battle, the cunning Hannibal had false campfires lit at Tuoro to lull his opponent into thinking his army was further away. Then he hid his men in the hills in such a way to sandwich the Roman army between his force and the lake below. As the Romans marched off in the morning in a heavy fog, the ambushers fell on them, forcing them to fight in open battle order rather than their normal battle array. Relentlessly the Romans were forced back to the lake — trapped by a superior surrounding force.

In just three hours, 15,000 Roman soldiers lay dead, including Flaminius, run through with a lance. The stream Sanguineto — Blood River — which runs through the site is said to have been named because it ran red with the blood of the slain for three days.

Hannibal's Second Punic War was to last another fifteen years. But it was to have great historic and social legacies, down to the present day. The fear that the defeat caused in Rome was to lead to the birth of the Roman Empire as a counter to future invasions. It also led to a large-scale abandonment of the land as enlisted small landowners were forced to sell their holdings to pay debts amassed during their army duties. The land, particularly in the south, fell into fewer but more economically powerful hands — a legacy I can look out onto from the windows of San Clemente.

Today, in summer, the shores of the lake below Tuoro sul Trasimeno resound to the sound of bumper cars, pleasure boats and disco music — not the clang of sword on sword, the screams of the dying or the hooves of the cavalry.

At the lakeside Lido di Tuoro stands no memorial to the dead but the Campo del Sole (Field of the Sun) with its remarkable 27 sculptured columns created in the 1980s as a sort of sculpture theme park. The columns, some as tall as four metres, are laid out in a spiral around a central solar symbol. On one visit to the Lido, Nancy and I had lunch at the Bar Ciao Ciao, one of the resort-type amenities available to the thousands of holiday-makers who flock there each summer. As we tried to conquer the Italian menu to decipher the marine life in its *insalata di mare* (seafood salad), waiters and waitresses gathered around us to offer advice. We must have passed some sort of test because as we left, we were handed a bottle of the establishment's own 'ciao ciao' labelled sparkling wine — an unexpected but much appreciated gesture, although we remained completely in the dark as to the reason for the generosity.

So this is my New World in the Old. Its frosts can be hard, its snows can be deep, its mists can be chilling and its winds cruel. But its warmth overrides these passing whims of nature — the warmth of its sun, of its culture, of its elegant beauty . . . and of the people who inhabit it.

CHAPTER FOUR

The Vendemmia of Brunello

AS AUTUMN TRIES lethargically to shake itself free of summer, the grapes are safely gathered and the *vendemmia* is at last over for another year on the slopes of Montalcino. It will be five years before the rest of Europe will be able to taste the results of our labours but we know that they will not be disappointed. This has been a bumper year for the annual grape harvest.

'My best yet,' says Austrian-born Harald Schwarz, the owner of the La Magia estate, one of the many wine estates nestled on the slopes of this historic fortress town in southern Tuscany. It is from these vineyards — and these alone — that what is arguably Italy's best and most famous wine finds its way to connoisseurs around the globe. The estate has had years when there have been more grapes and years when it has had better quality fruit. But never, says Harald, have the vines produced so many grapes of such high quality.

He and his German wife Gaby are delighted that the harvest

has taken under a week. When I was first asked to join the *vendemmia* by my German neighbour Ralph, who is the foreman at La Magia, I thought it would take up to two weeks. But we have worked quickly and well so not only have they got the grapes safely into the cellar but also saved substantially on their wage bill.

And there has been no rain. The harvesting has to stop if it rains as there will be too much moisture on the fruit to satisfy the quality control demands of Brunello.

It takes the full five years to mature the Brunello wines in their vast wooden barrels and to satisfy the rigorous quality control of the Denominazione di Origine Controllato e Garantita (DCOG) and the European Union. I am told that Brunello and Chianti (which is produced in the less wild territory of northern Tuscany, between Siena and Florence) are the only two Italian wines that meet the strict controls of the latter.

But our pleasure does not have to wait five years. As the last bunch of rich, sweet, juice-filled grapes is snipped from the fifteen hectares of vines we have our pleasure now, knowing that we have completed a hard job well. There are other emotions, too. Elation, relief, excitement, pride, exhaustion and, yes, pain. For this is hard work. In itself, the task is easy: walk along the rows of vines, snipping the bunches and placing them in plastic crates (*cassetta*) that hold about 20 kg. You work in pairs to help move the increasingly heavy *cassetta* as you proceed along the row. When your crate is filled, you place it under the vine for collection by tractor and trailer and simply pick up an empty case that has been pre-distributed along the pathway between the vine rows.

The procedure may sound easy but there is a range of conditions under which you work that have a cumulative effect so that, by day's end, you are totally exhausted. The La Magia estate's vines are planted in long rows, up to 250 metres down the hillside. So you walk up and down this slope all day. The path between the rows is rough, rocky and dusty — made worse as the harvest proceeds by the ripping tracks of the estate's bulldozer as it joins in with the collection of the *cassetta.*

You are employed to work for eight hours — literally. The work starts at 8 am, there is an hour for lunch, and it finishes at 5 pm. There are no in-between breaks for rest or refreshment. If you are lucky, you may come across a bottle of lukewarm water that one of the workers or 'bosses' has left at the end of a row. If you are luckier, there will still be some water in it.

The grapes grow at the bottom of the vines, at about thigh height. As a child, I once picked strawberries during school holidays and that was really back-breaking work. Grape harvesting does not require that full bending down, but you do have to crick your back a little to get at the fruit and, by the end of the day, your body is screaming for relief.

And then there is the heat. It may be the last week in September and a third of the way through the autumn season, but here in southern Tuscany the sun is still brutal as the day wears on. On my first day, one of my co-workers asked if I would prefer to work from 8 am–noon, then after lunch, 1 pm–5 pm. Or would I prefer to work five hours in the morning before the afternoon sun really begins to bite?

In his halting English, Armando explains: 'We try ask everybody. Most like work longer morning. Is cooler.' I readily agree and am glad I do, because 3 pm is the really tough part of the day. The sun is at its fiercest and you know you still have two hours to go.

Finally, for the younger men (and unfortunately I am included in this category) there is the shared task of collecting the filled *cassetta*. Two walk behind the trailer, one each side, to recover the crates from under the vines and heave them up and on to the trailer where two others stack them. This in itself is hard work but the final insult to your weary body is that the collection takes place going downhill and, once at the end of the row, you are forced to trudge through the heat and dust back up the hill again.

The compensations for all this toil are rich. At the most basic level, there is the sense of well-being from working hard in the open air and doing a job well. Then there is the knowledge that you are involved in a task that has been performed each year in this part of the world for centuries, a time-honoured tradition that remains much as it was two or more millennia ago. The romantic in me wants to believe that the hand-picking *vendemmia* in these last few years before a new millennium is a concession to this historical legacy. But Gaby brings me down to earth with a more pragmatic reason: 'We pick by hand to keep the grapes in good health. The modern machines just rip them up and they lose their goodness before they get to the press; we want to keep all that goodness before they get there.'

And the landscape is stunning. On my first morning, as I drive the 40 kilometres to the estate from my home, the sun rose above the hills just as I reached the bottom of the ascent up to Montalcino. The towers and turrets and walls of this ancient town on the very crest of the 567-metre hill glowed red. The surrounding lower landscape remained in the predawn shade. It was a sight I shall never forget. And on the following mornings, the red sun rising over the hills brought new, magical light effects to this most beautiful terrain.

One simple pleasure you could take during the long days in the vineyard was to pause to admire the remarkable view down the hillside, past the ordered rows of vines stretching into the valley below. There, in the middle distance, stands the Romanesque abbey of Sant'Antimo on a small rise. The abbey is so gracefully and naturally set into its environment that it takes on an almost mystical air. Today, the temple is home to a tiny band of Augustinian monks, who celebrate Mass daily with Gregorian chants that fill its vaulted walls with the centuries-old sound of prayer and devotion. And away in the distance loomed the imposing, sharply-pointed peak of Monte Amiata, the dominant geographical feature of this part of Tuscany. From its slopes, chestnut trees provided the raw material for the fleet of war galleys of Rome during the Second Punic War. And the Etruscan culture flourished under its shadow as far back as the fifth century BC.

'How long did you have to look to find such a beautiful site?' I asked Gaby one morning as we paired up for the harvesting.

'You don't look for a place like this. It finds you,' she replied. She told me that she and Harald had been asked to take over the fledgling vineyard some ten or eleven years ago, even though they had no experience growing grapes or producing wine.

'How could we refuse?' she said, gazing wistfully down the slopes, over the vines to Sant'Antimo, to the distant dark blue peaks of Monte Amiata that dominate the skyline.

But perhaps the richest reward to be had from the *vendemmia* came from the people I worked alongside through the harvest.

What a cheerful, friendly, efficient bunch! And such a mixed bag. I had looked forward to taking part from Ralph's first offer; eager, too, to actually do some serious work for the first time in nearly six months. Unfortunately the couple who introduced me to San Clemente would still be with me to show me the ropes over the first three days of the harvest. I could hardly waltz off during this time.

That night, Ralph called and asked if I would like to go along for half a day on the Saturday morning. I thanked him and set my alarm for the first time in months to make sure I would be on time for the early morning start.

I admit to having had a certain sense of nervousness. Would the other workers accept this non-Italian (and worse, non-Italian speaking) stranger from a faraway land? Would my days be spent in silence while they chattered and laughed and worked among themselves? Just how hard would the work be and would I be physically up to it? Would I be hopelessly out of my depth and be politely asked not to return? My worst fears were almost instantly realised. My first partner was one of the older men, who spoke no English. After a half-hour or so of smiles and silence, he wisely asked to have a partner he could talk to. So I was passed on to Franco, a young man in his twenties. Naturally he spoke no English either. But his brother, Armando, spoke a little so he joined me, again much to the relief of Franco.

Armando is an economics student at Siena University but he comes from the far south of Italy. He and Franco arrived each day with three other students from the university, Luca, also from the south, and two young women, one from the coast east of Rome and one from Sardinia.

I think at the outset the group of 25 gathered for the *vendemmia* did not know what to make of this stranger who came with the foreman and who spoke no Italian at all. But a tentative offering of friendship and acceptance came as we sat on the grass eating lunch on the first day. One of the students from Siena had a book about her home area in the south of Italy which she was showing to the others. Then she looked at me and offered me the chance to have a look. I grabbed the opportunity with a welcome relief; I couldn't, of course, read the words, but there were plenty of colour photographs of the towns in her part of Italy so I had some reason to show an interest.

And gradually, as they all discovered I was from New Zealand, their curiosity became aroused and it became clear that a good ten or so actually spoke some English.

'You are like a bird, flying from place to place,' said Marie-Therese, one of the students.

Then there was Heinz, the Austrian who came to the *vendemmia* 'for the fun of it'. He had a deeply-tanned, weather-beaten face that spoke of an outdoor, even nomadic life. And Mohammed, the young, swarthy, hook-nosed Algerian who had been living in France. He spoke very little English, but we were able to talk using French. Harald and Gaby spoke Italian, German and English. Sometimes as we worked Gaby would talk to me in German and to one of the Italians in English. 'It's very confusing,' she confessed.

At lunchtime, those of us not from the estate or Montalcino itself would sit in groups on the grass around the cellars. The packed lunches were as varied as the people. Some brought sandwiches, others fruit and cheese with a roll. The Italians unpacked little containers of cold pasta.

On 30 September, the last day of the *vendemmia* infused us all with a sense of eager anticipation and excitement. The hard work was coming to a close, we had become a close-knit group who worked steadily and well, and we were keen to finish the task. By 11.30 am we had completed harvesting the vines on the slopes below the cellars and the family home. Like a tasty morsel saved for the end of the meal, there remained only one small area on a flat piece of ground beside the entrance road to the property. As we straggled up to this last area, trudging wearily in the blazing midday sun, we paused briefly to gather, it seemed, the reserves to attack the final vines.

Most thought it would take at least two hours, but once we started a sense of excitement seemed to take control of all of us and we completed the task — and the *vendemmia* — in little over an hour. Weary but elated we gathered for lunch a few metres away in the estate's barbecue area where we all sat around a huge slab of flat rock that served as a table. The size of that one piece of rock can be appreciated when you realise that some 25 people were able to sit around it for the meal.

Someone had bought a case of ghastly sweet wine and some delicious Italian cakes (this is the country for sweet teeth), which we had after our own lunches. We all chipped in 5000 lire to help cover the cost. It was a time of camaraderie, photographs, swapping addresses and wallowing in shared and self-congratulations under the shade of the trees.

I was a little disappointed that Harald and Gaby had not supplied any 'goodies' for us, particularly as they were clearly pleased with our team effort. But Harald soon made a speech, which translated for me, informed us that we would all gather as their guests at a restaurant the following Friday night. Sadly for some, they would not be there. Heinz, for example, was returning to Austria the next day ('I was a painter of, how you say, buildings and houses, yes, last year. I don't know what I will do this year. Will I be back here next year? Who knows?'). Armando would be staying in Siena to be with his new American girlfriend. 'If I come to the dinner, what think she?'

Ralph and his wife drove me there, which was just as well as the restaurant was a long way from Montalcino, to the west, past the abbey of Sant'Antimo and deep into the foothills of Monte Amiata. I would have been hopelessly lost. Those of us who did not know the restaurant or the route to it gathered at a bar in Montalcino to follow one of the group who did.

As we quaffed wine from earthen jugs, nibbled at the antipasti and chose our pizzas, the same sense of comradeship we had shared at La Magia was still there. There was much laughter and good-humoured hectoring of Harald and Ralph, who organised and oversaw the work.

And that brought the *vendemmia* to an end for us. Who would be there next year? Will there be some other strange foreigner without the language who is checked over before being absorbed into the team? If so, I wish him or her well — not luck, because that's not needed; as long as you are willing and friendly you will be quickly adopted.

I shall not have the chance to taste the fruits of my labour for some years, yet. But I have a bottle of the 1991 Brunello vintage (the 1992 vintage, recently, was small and is no longer available) which I will share with Nancy when she comes to San Clemente next week. We will be in good company; according to *The Times* of London — and what better authority than the Old Thunderer? — this treasure from southern Tuscany is prized among others by Henry Kissinger and the late Frank Sinatra.

But in five years' time, wherever I am in the world, I will somehow find a bottle of the 1997 Brunello and raise a toast to my friends of the *vendemmia*. And to myself. I think I earned it on the sunny slopes of Montalcino.

CHAPTER FIVE

Nancy's First Visit

'YOU KNOW I could live here,' she said casually.

The hot autumn sun blazed down from the clear, sea-blue sky. The afternoon air was still and quiet. The Ca'de Sass was chilled perfectly, sparking and sparkling in the light. On the tray, the olives, the pecorino cheese, the *cinghiale* (wild boar) salami lay temptingly spread; the bright red tomatoes glistened with olive oil and sent out the sharp green tang of freshly-chopped basil leaves.

Nancy had arrived at San Clemente less than an hour before and we both wanted her to absorb the serenity and beauty of my new home.

She was my first visitor and arrived halfway through October, as the leaves of the holm oaks, acacias and other trees in the woods around me turned brown, gold and red.

Before Nancy arrived, my time at San Clemente had been one of wonder at the beauty around me, awe at the architecture and history of the ancient hilltop towns and sheer astonishment at the drama and ever-changing colours of the landscape of southern Tuscany.

But her visit unleashed a completely new range of emotional and personal feelings that I have never experienced before. I made important decisions and leapt mental hurdles that had affected both myself and my relationship with others throughout my life. It was as if I had reached the end of a search spanning nearly half a century and entered into a whole new world. It was an astounding week of personal pleasure and personal revelation.

That first afternoon, after our drive through Le Crete from Florence, I dismissed her comment about being able to live at San Clemente as the immediate, understandable reaction of someone seeing the house and its environment for the first time. I, too, had been overwhelmed by its beauty when I first saw it in daylight.

So I simply put her thought aside and prepared to savour the coming seven days. By the end of that week, though, that early comment was to become an exciting reality as we decided a future for ourselves together.

It was the most sensational week for both of us. Each day we found a new pleasure that intensified the happiness we felt in each other's company — the foot baths at Bagno Vignoni, the beauty of Pienza, the majesty of the Duomo at Siena and Florence, the awe-inspiring first glimpse of Il Campo at Siena, the views and steep narrow alleys of Cortona, the first sight of Florence's historic town centre and the Ponte Vecchio spanning the River Arno . . .

It was a privilege and a joy to show Nancy my new world. But it was this path of personal discovery that was to make the week the most remarkable and memorable of both our lives, as we agreed later.

Back in England I had suggested that we each compile a list

of our main loves and hates in life so we could talk through them when she came to Tuscany. My motivation was simple; I did not want to fall into the mistakes of the past. Rather, I wanted Nancy to know everything about me — my fears and anxieties, my insecurities, what brought me enjoyment and pleasure. At the same time, I wanted to know all about her. I was determined that if this was to be not only a successful relationship but a true love, then I wanted to feel no fears about communicating any thoughts to her. To my delight, Nancy accepted the idea with enthusiasm and, while I awaited her visit, we worked on our lists and exchanged them by post.

We each approached the project with great seriousness, separately aware that this was an important milestone in our relationship. And throughout our week together, it became an emotional marathon, draining us mentally and physically but exhilarating our souls as we laid bare those innermost feelings we normally hide from the world.

Each night after dinner we would sit in the lounge and take turns to talk about one of the loves or hates we had listed. For my part, I was completely committed to opening myself up emotionally no matter what the cost.

This was a relationship that was barely two months old; others I have had have lasted more than 20 years without me baring my soul in this way.

It was, for both of us, a voyage of discovery into often uncharted waters, neither of us knowing where a new subject might take us. Some were relatively quick and easy but others took an hour or more to talk through as we sometimes painfully delved into our consciousness. We laughed a lot and we cried a lot, but always there was the sense of trust and honesty; we were both wanting to give our souls to each other.

Through our separate lists we discovered not only the pleasures of our lives and how much of these we had in common — friends and family, cooking and entertaining, shared musical tastes — but quite separate 'Top 10' loves (although when we went through them we could agree that they were things we could both take pleasure in): sunsets at the beach, drinking fine wine, being warm, going into a warm house in winter with the aroma of a roast dinner cooking in the oven, the traditions of Christmas, being loved, giving love and just being in love . . .

Our 'Top 10' hates in many ways reflected personal events in our pasts that had dug deeply into our psyches. These were the issues that were often the most painful to talk about. They brought old insecurities to the surface and opened emotional wounds that had, in some cases, remained deeply hidden since childhood. The trust and openness with which we were prepared to talk about these things amazed us.

I made some important decisions that I had been backing away from. The most significant one was to decide that this love was so right, so strong and so good that any hesitancy about getting married again simply vanished. Nancy decided to ask about taking leave of absence from her job to come to San Clemente for two or three years. These were not insignificant matters but they seemed the most obvious ones in the world.

Nancy was later to write to her family: 'In the less than two months I have known him, we have communicated our loves and fears so freely that we know each other better than many couples do in a lifetime.'

But her visit was much more than a voyage of discovery about each other — it was also great fun. I introduced Nancy to the places and people I had so far encountered in my still-brief sojourn. And we went to the new places that I had avoided until then so we could enjoy discovering them together.

I took her back to La Magia on the slopes of Montalcino to show her where I had laboured in the sun during the *vendemmia*. Then we travelled on to Abbazia Sant'Antimo that I had looked down on during those September days. And then to the spa at Bagno Vignoni and to Pienza. On another day, we drove to Lake Trasimeno, where Hannibal inflicted his huge defeat on the Roman army. From there we went up the steep, winding road to the ancient town of Cortona, made famous in another recent book about Tuscany. Its steep alleys and steps would pull us back time after time. From the ramparts at one of the main historic gates to the old town we could see our own *i monti* directly across the flat plain of the Valdichiana.

We went walking in the woods beneath the ruins and tourist apartments of the 700-year-old castle of Montelifre, on the other side of *i monti* to San Clemente. We got hopelessly lost and had to backtrack. On the way, Nancy decided to try one of the olives on the trees in the field. 'They're really bitter, you won't like it,' I said with the smugness of recent experience. But she insisted and it took a good hour for that bitter taste to disappear from her palate.

That experience aside, we ate well — at the nearby Le Logge fish restaurant where I had been entertained by Carlo on my first arrival. It offered a set menu, with five antipasto dishes coming out in succession, then the *primo* course and finally the *secondo*. The antipasti included deep-fried potato and cheese gnocchi, octopus slices, scampi and prawns with a tasty lemon/oil sauce, and a cold mousse of cod on a lettuce leaf.

The *primo* course was prawns, calamari and crayfish with tagliatelle. The *secondo* was steamed cod offset by the sharp taste of arugula.

I had dessert — a creamy mousse with warm, thick chocolate sauce on top. We both drank the liqueur called Amaro, from Sicily.

Later in the week we ate out again, at our local Trequanda restaurant, Conte Matto, just behind the main piazza. Although a Friday night, it was very quiet. But the food was again excellent — a selection of antipasti (pâté, small cocktail-like onions, grilled eggplant in oil, sun-dried tomatoes, hard-boiled eggs, prosciutto, salami). I also had the local wild boar ragoût and Nancy the grilled duck. Both, we agreed, were excellent.

And I cooked at San Clemente for Nancy. On our last afternoon, while she painted *i monti* in the sun, I prepared roast lamb with rosemary and garlic. She was amazed that I made gravy to go with it. 'You make gravy? That's it. Wait till I tell my mother you make gravy. You're in there, definitely!' This was certainly encouraging, but it seemed no big deal as I had been making gravy for years.

And so we moved towards the last day, the day we had been dreading all week. As Friday, then Saturday arrived we began admitting to each other how unhappy we were that Nancy had to leave and how much we were hating the prospect of our last Sunday together while we waited for her flight from Florence airport. Memories of our earlier parting in England lingered over us like death.

We left San Clemente early so we would have time to see the historic centre of the city of the Medici, the Renaissance, Michelangelo and Dante. Our first view from the Piazzale de Michelangelo, on the tree-lined Viale Galileo Galilei, was as stunning to us as it has been to the countless millions of travellers and tourists who have first glimpsed those majestic towers and turrets and domes on the flat valley floor below. The Arno with the Ponte Vecchio that Hitler spared from destruction as the Allies advanced north (the only bridge over the Arno not to be blown up by the retreating Germans), the minaret-like turreted tower of the Uffizi and, dominating the entire city, the enormous dome of the Duomo, Florence's huge cathedral . . . the sight was breathtaking and humbling.

We drove down into the city, across the Ponte San Nicolo, up the five-lane Viale Giovanni Amendola and back down the

Viale della Giovine Italia before turning right to park along the Arno itself.

We walked along the banks to the Uffizi, described as one of the world's great art galleries, its long, thin central courtyard flanked by the high arcaded buildings that open out at the far end onto the broad expanse of the Piazza della Signoria with its famed statues and fountains. We strolled on to the Ponte Vecchio, equal to the Duomo as representing the soul of Florence, for me at least. For the last 1000 years a bridge has spanned the Arno here, where it is perhaps 150 metres wide. The tiny shops that line both sides are a mecca for lovers of gold and silver jewellery.

The day was beautiful and both Nancy and I were anxious to spend as much time together as possible. So rather than be distracted by the great works of art and architecture that surrounded us, we sat instead at a table outside one of the cafés that line two sides of the piazza and spent the early afternoon people-watching. We talked, drank cold beers, soaked up the sun, watched the world go by and revelled in each other before leaving for the airport.

We decided Nancy would come back in November, less than three weeks away. And that I would fly with her to New Jersey for Christmas and New Year with her family and friends.

By the week's end I had come to understand that those six short words she said on the afternoon of her arrival were no idle daydream. With her 20 years of service, she should surely qualify for two or even three years leave of absence. After that, who knew? More, who cared? And later still? Later, we decided, would take care of itself.

So we had a semblance of a future mapped out, removing the uncertainty about how we would engineer a life together between Italy, England and the United States.

If the future was cheery, that first night after Nancy left was bleak. It was a lonely drive back to Trequanda in the dark to be welcomed by an empty, echoing villa that just hours before had been filled with her love and happiness.

Nancy had asked me two things soon after she arrived. What made this relationship so different to the others I had had? And would I tape her a message so she could have my voice with her when we were apart?

This is the beginning of the message she took back to England.

'Probably the biggest difference is the one I can't point at and say, "That's it, that's what it is." It's an intangible thing, a feeling, an emotion. I've just never known that someone is so perfect for me in such a quick timeframe. It has just felt so right and so good and so strong right from the start.'

Later, when we reflected on our week together and our love for each other in letters and other messages, I added, 'You filled San Clemente with love and warmth and happiness. You made it feel like a real home for the first time since I got here. I have so much to thank you for. For taking me into your life and heart. For making me feel so special. For accepting my love . . . What memories I have! And what memories we have to share.'

Nancy's reply was equally revealing. 'It was a pleasure being your special guest. It felt so comfortable living with you and being in your presence [that] upon returning to Bath I have a sense of peace and calm . . . You have helped me become the person I've longed to be and for that I sincerely thank you. You can't imagine how happy I am with myself and my new life you have given me . . .'

Nancy also sent me the final words of a letter to her parents that she had started at San Clemente, introducing the new man in her life.

'I have never been so proud to bring someone home to meet you. I want you to know all about him and our intense feelings for each other. He is my love, lover, best friend, soulmate and guardian angel. It doesn't get any better than this!'

Or could it?

CHAPTER SIX

A-Hunting We Will Go

IN AUTUMN THE rising sun is greeted by the sound of death crackling and echoing through the woods and fields that surround San Clemente.

It is the hunting season and a time for dying.

From sunrise to sunset, the wild game and birds that make *sotto i monti* their home are, literally, fair game for the hundreds of Italians who come to display their manhood slung over their shoulders. And they do not want for choice.

This is an extraordinarily rich world of wildlife. Roe deer, fallow deer, hares, squirrels, weasels, martens, wild boar, porcupines (some weighing as much as 15 kg), polecats, badgers, water voles and large green lizards are just some representatives of the animal and reptile kingdom. The bird life is as diverse. Hoopoos, curlews, magpies, jackdaws, ravens, cuckoos, nightingales, robins, thrushes, pheasants, doves, harriers, buzzards, red and green woodpeckers and pilgrim hawks mate, nest, raise their young and try to survive in this environment.

During the day, I can hear the squealing of the wild boar. At night, the crickets and owls come out to play. There is one owl who has discovered the joy of screeching in the tree outside my window at 5.30 am each morning. And throughout these months and into the New Year, I hear the sharp crack of hunting rifles and the heavy 'whoomp' of shotguns.

Sundays are the busiest days for death here, when it becomes almost a factory production line. It is the day when the city folk come to play alongside the locals. They are easy to identify. Their number plates show homes in Milan, Rome and Florence and their elegant hunting kit is still shiny and new as if just unpacked in the back of the BMWs and Mercedes and Alfa Romeos they have driven from their expensive apartments in the chic cities of Italy. It is a dress uniform and is very correct. It proclaims wealth and status and manliness — a macho equivalent of the Burberry set in England. The locals, at least, have the good sense to dress down in jeans or rough wool trousers and rugged, practical shirts and jerseys.

There are midweek days when I am spared the sound of death, days when the hunters are barred from their trade, perhaps days of rest and recovery for the wildlife. But on other days the ritual begins as soon as the sun rises. And if Sunday is the busiest it is also the most poignant and redolent with irony. For as the bells of the abbeys and churches in the small towns just over the hills sound their call for Mass, fusillades of gunshots ripple over, up and down the ridges and valleys that surround me. This amphitheatre of death becomes like a natural music chamber, playing a macabre and mournful melody on a day when resurrection, faith and hope are celebrated.

Sometimes there is a rapid burst of three or four shots, sometimes just one sharp 'crack'. Sometimes the firing is distant, over a ridge line or high in the Bosconi, 'big woods' that drape *i monti*. And sometimes the shots are so close that I jump with alarm, particularly with the sound of a high-calibre rifle.

For they roam at will, these hunters. There are no trespass laws in Italy and anyone is free to walk through fields, woods, pastures as they wish. The only exception is where there is a fence three metres or more high. But even that is taken as an affront to this 'right' that the hunters so nonchalantly assume. Farther down my road there is one such fence; David, who introduced me to this world, tells me one day as we drive by: 'That won't last long; they'll knock it down or put a hole in it. They don't like to think that they can't go where they want.'

So they tramp the fields and stalk the woods, serene in the knowledge that it is their God-given right. In fact it is their Mussolini-given right, one that has long outlasted Il Duce.

I am told by an English woman who has been living here for some ten years that they are not allowed to fire a weapon within 150 metres of a building and that they must ask permission (or rather tell) the inhabitant or owner of the property that they will be coming to shoot on the land.

'Hah, never happened yet,' she snorts with contempt. Certainly, it never happened at San Clemente in those first autumn months.

'So how long does the hunting season last?' I ask in my newcomer's ignorance.

'God knows. It never seems to stop. There's always something that seems to be in season.'

That was not encouraging news.

'There seem to be an awful lot of them. How much does a licence cost?' I ask again.

'Next to nothing, dirt cheap. It's used as a vote-catcher by the local Communists — give the locals cheap hunting and get their votes at the elections. They're much more expensive in other regions where the Communists don't govern and so cannot set the regional licence fees.'

And in this way I learn more about how the Communists (since the collapse of the Soviet Union, Reformed Communists) dominate this part of Italy politically and have done so since the immediate post-war years when local Communist partisans took control from the defeated Fascist and other splinter groups.

Hunting votes with cheap hunting licences. Politicians are the same the world over, I suppose.

The woman recalls how she was pilloried by locals who thought her an uppity foreigner for daring to complain when the hunters came too close to her home and terrified her pet dogs.

Those from the towns and cities are the worst sort of hunter, completely ignorant of the simple, commonsense rules of a rural community. They leave gates open, they cut fencing to make holes rather than climb over it, they dig trenches under the fences so they don't snag their elegant new outfits on the wire. And they make a terrible din as they stumble through the woods, crashing through bushes, cursing as they trip, whistling and calling their dogs, shouting greetings to companions if they have them.

The dogs, too, are great sport to watch. Italians are notorious for their neglect of their dogs. Perhaps it is not a deliberate neglect, just a total failure to understand what dogs need, how they react and how they should be trained. Most of the dogs that the city folk in particular bring to the fields and woods around me are utterly hopeless. Many are driven encased in small cages in the boot of a car or on a small trailer towed behind it. When they are let loose, these poor animals who may well have spent their entire year locked up in a big city apartment, go wild with the sense of freedom. They scamper about the fields and through the wood, tails wagging rapturously as if they have finally reached some sort of canine paradise. They completely ignore the shouts, whistles and irate abuse of their owners. As one hunter walked across a field, his dog blissfully running free, a cock pheasant calmly stalked out of the woods behind him, right past him and into one of the hedgerows that line my road.

Sometimes master and dog walk down the road past my drive. My faithful Molly barks sternly at them and rushes to defend our patch. But she is really too much of a lady and too old for these young upstarts to pay her too much attention. So they bound into our grounds, sniffing and smelling and delightedly exploring this whole new world that has been presented to them. The helpless owner just stares at me from the road with a silly grin on his face, with absolutely no control over his charge. Only when the dog has decided that it has had enough are the two reunited again.

And off they go, banging and crashing their way through the woods, the dog barking excitedly and surely scaring away any sensible game within 500 metres.

It is not uncommon to meet hunting types in cars on my road, searching for dogs they have lost in the woods. Other hunters try to counter this possibility by attaching bells to the collars of their dogs. Very clever. It means the hunter can easily keep track of his dog by listening to the tinkling it makes as it roams the woods. And so can any game that might be in the vicinity. At the sound of the warning bell, it can quickly make itself scarce — the tinkling of bells is, after all, hardly a natural call of the wild. So the hunter gets to go home with his dog, but most certainly with no game in his bag.

I have great scepticism about the hunting prowess of most of those who come to *sotto i monti* to kill. I have additionally no little nervousness about their awareness of my home, my dog and, not least, myself. I have no idea how well trained with weapons these hunters are, nor how excited they might get if by chance they spy a game animal in line of sight with San

Clemente and let loose a volley of bullets in their eagerness to kill. One day out driving I passed a track leading into some heavy woods. On the roadside were some 20-30 cars, presumably hunters who knew a good site. Nothing would have induced me to go down that track!

And then one Sunday in November, I am witness, from my own windows, to the most bizarre hunting scene I have ever seen. At 11 am, a convoy of hunters invades my road. There are about 50 cars and, I suppose, some 70 hunters.

Half stop about halfway along my lane, the one that leads to the road to Trequanda from San Clemente. The other half arrive on my doorstep, where their cars line the road as if I am throwing some large party.

They are armed with rifles, shotguns, picnic lunch boxes, folding camping stools and — this I find astonishing — umbrellas! In New Zealand, such hunters would be laughed out of the bush and back to their towns and cities.

And so they march into the field along my fenceline and along hedgerows and pockets of woods that slope up from my backyard. Then they proceed to set up their stools and their lunches and their umbrellas around the perimeter of the ploughed field that is only just now beginning to show signs of sprouting seed.

And there they wait, grimly staring into the field. Yes, into the field! I am no hunter, but even in my ignorance it takes little imagination to suppose that wild boar and deer will not miraculously appear in the middle of a stark-naked field. They are more likely to emerge from the trees and undergrowth towards which these hunters have their backs turned.

It takes little imagination to envisage the carnage if the miracle occurs and a game animal magically appears out there in the middle of their excited gun sights. The poor beast will, of course, be shredded so finely that there will be only a thimbleful of minced game meat left for each hunter to take home proudly to his adoring wife. But more to the point, I can imagine the carnage of all the bullets that miss and go whizzing across the field to where other hunters are aiming and firing back . . . It is the same as the classic gag where the firing squad stands in a circle and the victim ducks when the guns are fired.

These dudes are dressed in the best camouflage jackets that money can buy as they stand and sit in the gloom of an overcast and showery afternoon. Will a hunter notice an animal out of the corner of his eye, wheel, raise his weapon and fire, not even seeing his camouflaged companion next down the line?

Molly and I stay indoors all afternoon, well away from the windows apart from an occasional bemused peek. Gradually, and well before the official close of play at sunset, they drift away — cold, dispirited and without a trophy to parade. Who are they, this invading army? Where have they come from? Have they ever been hunting or held a gun in their hands before? How did they discover my little piece of Tuscany? I have no idea, but perhaps I should thank them for the entertainment they have provided.

Another day six boars ran across the open field beside the house, unnoticed and unmolested by the large party of hunters crashing and yelling through the undergrowth in the woods. They arrived in the morning and spent the day moving up and down the ridge line. I can only assume it was some sort of beating exercise because of the terrific din that rang through the woods all day. Their dogs barked and yelped continuously, those with bells adding their ringing to the clamour.

It sounded like a war zone. Gunshots rang out throughout the day. Occasionally a crack would be followed by a pained squeal from one of the dogs, perhaps mistaken for a wild boar. Late afternoon, many of the hunters came walking by the house on the way back to their cars. None had any discernible game in their hands or slung from their belts. I wondered if they blazed away at trees and bushes just to get the smell of powder on their clothes to impress the folks back home.

There are, obviously, good hunters who know how to handle a rifle or shotgun properly, who know how to train their dogs and keep them under control, who know how to stalk in silence. But I have only seen one in my time here so far. One morning a middle-aged man walked past San Clemente with a cheery wave and greeting. Over the next hour I heard three rifle shots close by in the woods. And then he returned. As he passed the drive he turned to me and waved, grinned again and lifted his coat tail to reveal three big hares tied to his belt. He was clearly a man who knew this business of death very well.

And so for these long autumn months and into winter I will know that death stalks these hills and fields. But as the cold weather has come to San Clemente and this wild part of Tuscany there has been a marked drop in the reports of gunshots. Perhaps as winter bites, it will come to a virtual stop compared to the almost constant fire during those balmy days of September when the sun rose like a fireball away to the east over Valdichiana and still had the power to bake the ground. That is possibly the last laugh the 'fair game' that lives and dies around me has — these are fair-weather hunters only. If the birds and animals that live in these woods can survive those first warm weeks of autumn they will be left in peace to continue the cycle of their lives.

CHAPTER SEVEN

The Pressing of the Oil

ELARIO, MY NEW friend and mentor, has a contented smile on his grandfatherly face as he gazes at the steady stream of yellow-gold, viscous, translucent liquid, glistening richly in the glare of an overhead light.

'Is good colour. Is good year. Is good oil,' he predicts with the experience of a lifetime in this hilly terrain.

Later, after tasting the first of countless bruschetta (thick toasted slices of bread rubbed with garlic and doused with warm olive oil) he will enjoy in the coming year, he confirms what the colour and his own knowledge have already told him.

'Is beautiful colour. Is very beautiful taste. Very sweet, no bitter.'

And so Elario can face the coming year with enjoyable expectation, knowing that this year's harvest of the *olio di oliva* is worthy of this region's reputation for producing, in his words, 'the best olive oil in all of Italy'.

It is no mean boast; the extra-virgin oil, *nuovo di podere*, from the hills and valleys of this little part of the world is renowned for its quality, taste, colour, smell, nutritional value and low acidity.

All the oil that flows from these hills has the right to be known as extra-virgin. In Italy, any oil with an acidity content of less than one per cent can boast this proud appellation. But the acidity content of my local oil can be as low as 0.14 per cent.

The high altitude of the hills (from 400 to 500 metres above sea level), high latitude and distance from the coast (we are virtually in the centre of the Italian 'boot') means that there is no need to spray insecticide to protect against the olive fly found in the coastal areas and that there is a low yield per acre, thus providing a better quality.

The absence of industry and the need for pesticides, combined with the large tracts of forested land, also means there is no toxic residue in the fruit. There is also a low proportion of peroxides, protecting the consumer against oxidation and consequent ageing. The olives are also cold pressed and there is no need for chemical additives because of their natural qualities.

The respect and value that the locals like Elario have placed on the land, the trees and the fruit over the centuries is vital to this formula that produces this age-old food. But it is the nature of the soil and the climatic conditions of the area that he points to as the most important contributor to the quality.

'Here there is a lot of stone in the earth. This means rainwater disappears quickly and earth stays very dry. Where there is water and humidity, is not very good for olive quality.'

Even so, quality can vary from season to season.

'Like grapes and wine, if not much summer rain, olives are smaller and have not so much water, but more oil, which makes better oil.'

Elario's own olive grove is slowly recovering from a severe winter in the 1980s that killed many of his trees. 'So cold that olives froze on tree.'

He replanted and gradually the production has been returning, 100 kg one year, 200 the next, 600 the year after. With his peasant farming heritage, nothing goes to waste. The dead trees are cut up for firewood — 'very good wood for burning' — and stored in his basement with the wine and olive flagons and his tools. From there, using a small ladle and funnel, he fills my five-litre jar with the precious liquid. There is even an enormous wooden barrel for ageing the wine.

'I try to sell [the barrel] but no one wants wood, just steel and metal today. But this makes very, very good wine,' he says, rapping it with his knuckles.

So this year's dry summer has produced a particularly high quality oil and on the last day of the harvest season I set out to witness the small black fruit become the rich, delicious liquid that gleams with such magnificent colour. It is the last of the crops to be harvested for the year and, throughout November, the fruit have been gathered from the countless olive trees that line the roadsides, sit in garden groves or fall in ordered ranks down the southern Tuscan hillsides that surround me.

On this last day of autumn, the sky has been unplugged for the last 36 hours and my metalled road has become a swift mountain stream in places, with no sign of the road's surface visible under the dun-coloured flow. But just seven kilometres away, in the tiny, ancient hilltop town of Montisi, the stream of oil has been flowing for a month, up to 24 hours a day at the height of the harvest.

Now the flow of the dark fruit into the *frattoio*, the oil mill, is slowing and the two-centimetre-wide stream of oil only runs for, perhaps, twelve hours a day, says Signor Talini who has overseen this family business for the last 40 years. When the harvest is finished and the giant grinding stones finally stop for another year in ten days or so, this single olive oil press will have produced some 100,000 litres of oil from the 500 tonnes of fruit gathered by hand or special comb from the slopes, hilltops and valley floors that surround it.

First, though, I drive to Castelmuzio where Elario and his brothers, Leonidi and Vittorio, are packing the produce from five properties into sacks to take to the *frattoio*. Earlier, I had seen them hand-picking the olives from the trees in the garden of my neighbour, Airdrie.

At this stage, the olives are not yet ripe, even though leaving them until they are would produce more oil.

'When olives are ripe, you get dark oil, not best colour. Does not affect other quality, only colour is different, but goldish-green oil from not ripe olives is better.' He explains that the darker oil does not command as high a price as the oil from the unripened fruit.

So it is a delicate balancing act and a form of quality control. Unripened fruit means less oil but a higher price and better quality. And the region takes great pride in maintaining its reputation for producing the finest quality oil — an annual conference on olive oil is held each year in my town of Trequanda.

Elario pays particular attention to delicately removing the fruit and placing them in the wicker half-basket tied to his waist, the same collection method that has been used for centuries and known as *brucatura*.

'Is important not get too many leaves in with olives. Too many leaves make oil taste very bitter if in with pressing. Oil is then no good.'

And later, at the *frattoio*, he points out crops from other farmers which, even to my inexperienced eyes, have an abundance of the silvery-green leaves contrasting with the black of the fruit. This seems to me to be sloppy. There are three stages at which the leaves can be separated from the fruit — during the picking and then at the mill where, first, the crop is passed under a large extractor fan before plunging down a chute for washing and rinsing in the downstairs production room, the last opportunity to discard extraneous matter.

I notice another sign of careless cropping at this last stage before the olives and whatever leaves remain are crushed — muddy water and gravel. This suggests that the particular grower has not been too worried that his olives have had contact with the ground during the harvest. Such irreverent treatment of the olives is anathema to Elario and to all olive oil authorities.

'If are on the ground, affects the taste very very bad. Must not touch the earth,' he insists as my education continues.

For the same reason, the gathered crop is stored in raised wooden trays to keep them dry and so avoid fermentation.

'Is best to pick olives and take to *frattoio* on same day,' says Elario. But because he has his five separate olive crops to gather together, this is not possible and they must be stored in a dry environment, in their trays, until all five crops are together to take to the mill.

He has his own crop, of course, and it represents the largest proportion of the fruit the brothers will sack and take to Montisi for pressing — some 600 of the total 935 kg they deliver.

His harvest has come from the 120 trees he owns on a hectare of land about a kilometre from his home. His brother Vittorio has brought his own crop from the coastal city of Livorno where he now lives. Then there is the crop of the other brother, Leonidi, who lives not far away in the town of Torrita di Siena. There are even some 'Irish' olives here — from the grove of Airdrie, my neighbour. And finally there is a small crop

— about 35 kg — from another grower in the town of Petroio on the road between my home and Elario's.

The olives have been stored in the loft of Elario's garage, across the narrow street from his home. As I arrive, the three brothers have begun putting them into sacks for the trip to Montisi. It is a cold, showery day, but the work is labour intensive and warming. Elario proudly shows me his self-invented system for transferring the olives from the loft to the street below — one brother above uses a bucket to scoop up the olives from the aeration trays and then pours them into a plastic basin with a plastic pipe. Like downpipes in the guttering system of a house, these simply descend to street level where the sacks are placed for the bagging. To regulate the flow when each sack is filled and needs replacing, he has a shaped piece of tin which he can insert into a slot in the pipe. This shuts off the flow until a new sack is put in place.

'I invent system,' he says proudly, explaining that before devising this gravity feed production line he used to tote the sacks up the 20 or so narrow stairs, fill each sack with some 40 kg of olives and then carry it down the stairs over his shoulder.

The task finished, we load up the vehicles for the drive to Montisi. At the *frattoio*, each arriving crop is weighed and separately stored to await its turn for processing.

First, the fruit is passed under the extractor fan to remove leaves, dirt, twigs and so on. Then it is sent down a chute into the production line where it is washed, then crushed before proceeding into a large pressing basin where two huge grinding stones rotate to grind the olives — flesh, skin, stones and whatever else remains — into a glutinous black paste.

It is a curious blend of ancient custom and modern technology. The grinding stones — each about 1.5 metres across and half a metre deep and weighing about two tonnes — are merely larger versions of those used by peasants to grind their harvest two or more millennia ago. But today they are powered by motors and the rest of the production line is similarly controlled by modern machinery.

After the grinding, which takes about fifteen minutes, the paste then passes into an open pipe where it is heated while kneading blades, like those used for making dough, churn it. This process is designed to warm the oil in the paste so it is more fluid for the extraction processes to come.

The next stage is the removal of the waste from the liquid. The waste — the solid material that is left from the skins and stones and other matter — is piped to an outside storage area. It will be sent to be processed into manure or animal feed. In older days, when the whole process was less efficient and powerful, the waste would still hold residues of oil and water and would be further refined for using in by-products like oil for canned sardines or tuna. But today the process is so effective that there is no moisture left.

The liquid extracted is still a mixture of the oil and water. So the next stage is to separate them through two centrifuge processes. The water, which is very acidic, is simply waste.

And so the final product — the precious olive oil — is all that is left. After a final filtering stage, it runs in its small glowing stream into the containers for the farmers, orchardists and small landholders to take home and store for the year. Elario explains that he uses large glass or metal containers to store the 35–40 litres he will keep for himself (friends and afficionados who know of the care he devotes to his trees and its harvest will buy the remaining 70 or so litres he does not need).

'I used to use terracotta but now they use, how you say, petrol-based chemicals in making the pots, not water like old days. So gives oil a bad taste.'

And, finally, the 'real oil' from the expert on how best to

enjoy the extra-virgin oil, and get the maximum taste and scent from it.

'On bruschetta. Cut slices of bread and put under heat. Not under flame, burns bread. Not in oven, makes bread dry. Under grill. Must be thick to make outside hard like toast but inside still soft.

'Straight from heat, rub garlic on both sides. Then pour lot of oil on both sides, or dip into oil in bowl. Must have lot of oil. Add salt. And more garlic, enough to burn your mouth.

'Is beautiful taste.'

Oh yes.

CHAPTER EIGHT

At War with Nature

I AM IN the front line of a dirty, dangerous war here in San Clemente. *Sotto i monti* is a perilous place for the unwary, despite its beauty. There are dangers lurking in the woods, in the air, on the ground, under the ground and even deep within the earth's crust. There are pests, parasites, poisoners and pricklers. There are flying things, digging things, hiding things, running things and scuttling things. There are things that can bite, sting, scratch, poison, infect, gore, cut, prick and otherwise torment you. There are tusks, antlers, spines, quills, nippers, claws, fangs, barbs, thorns, prickles, bristles, sharp teeth and stingers.

One learns quickly to keep up one's guard.

If I wander in the woods, I am at risk from some fiercely protective mother boar. Or I may stumble on a 15 kg porcupine. But these are the least of my worries; the reason I seldom wander alone is fear of some demented hunter armed with a powerful rifle.

No, it is close around the home that I have to be wary.

There are horseflies, houseflies and blowflies. Walking ants, flying ants and stalking ants can give you a vicious bite as you sit enjoying the midday sun with lunch, a cold beer and an English-language newspaper.

There are hornets, wasps, bumblebees and honey bees. Some, like the hornets, are capable of really taking a dislike to me and attacking *en masse*, which would be very serious news indeed. I had not been stung by a wasp for years until I arrived at San Clemente. In the first two days, I was stung twice.

There are creatures that buzz, hum, crackle, drone or whine as they circle around me. More alarmingly, there are things that I have never seen before but which I know can be a serious threat to my well-being. Two names spring shiveringly to mind: vipers and scorpions.

I have never seen a snake in the wild, let alone one that can actually kill me. Nor have I seen a scorpion.

'Not to worry,' said the person introducing me to what was rapidly becoming this place of pestilence. 'I never saw one of either in the seven years I was here. There was a grass snake by the front door but they're harmless. Just watch where you put your hands. If there's a pile of old timber or broken tiles, give them a rattle with a stick first, that'll scare them off. They're more frightened of you than you of them.'

I can just see it — an innocent hand mistakenly slips into a viper's nest and all the poor, timid, frightened reptile is going to do is shriek with alarm. Around here there are a lot of piles of old timber and broken tiles, empty flower pots and pruned tree limbs for legions of vipers and scorpions to lurk just waiting for me to forget to give them a rattle beforehand.

'You can get an antidote pack against the venom, but it's a hassle. You've got to keep it chilled and it costs a lot and its probably just as easy and effective to give someone a ring.'

In my fractured Italian, while I'm dying?

I have discovered a small handbook in the house. It has a lovely round photograph of a viper in aggressive mode. Its title is *Vipere Italiane*. It has a sub-title: *Vademecum 'SCLAVO' per chi ama vivere all'aria aperta*. I think this means 'Keeping yourself alive'.

The first page inside has four photos — a falcon, a hedgehog, a pig and a turkey. I have no idea what these are meant to tell me about snakes. Further into the booklet, there are close-up photos of vipers. They have sly, cunning, almost maliciously delighted eyes. There is a diagram of exactly where the venom will come from and how it will travel through the snake to its fangs when they dig deep into me. There is even a photo of a viper leering and grinning with a horn-like protuberance at its snout.

Later still there are photos of people in situations that I assume are meant to be places where vipers might wait in ambush. Some look terrifyingly like the places around here.

And, lastly, there is the comforting sight of someone — I can't tell whether it's a man or woman but it hardly seems to matter — tying a tourniquet around his or her upper arm and then administering an injection to his or her lower arm. I rehearse the situation. I've just been bitten by a poisonous snake. I'm going to calmly walk back into the house and search for the first aid kit. Oh, that's right, silly me, it's in the fridge, but where's the damned needle? I'll tell you where I'll really be — in the car, roaring up my road to neighbours at about 160 km/h.

One morning I discovered a round hole in the side lawn that looked *exactly the right size for a poisonous snake to slither into*. Being just two metres from my kitchen window, this seemed pretty accurately to fit the book's warning about dangers in one's 'immediate vicinity'. Of course there were no signs up to advise 'viper's home' or 'grass snake's nest'. This placed me in a quandary. Not being at all familiar with the snake kingdom (since snakes do not exist in New Zealand), I had no way of telling whether it actually was a snake hole, and if so, what type of snake had taken a liking to my lawn.

I mentioned my discovery to Carlo.

'Oh, that will be Marta,' he said cheerily.

Marta?

'Yes, she likes to live around the property. It's OK, though, she's harmless, just a grass snake. That's what I call her. She likes to live under the house where there's a big open area. But we blocked off the hole by the front door so now she just turns up around the place. We've met several times, often in the garage. She moves one way and I move the other.'

So now I have a squatter called Marta. A snake.

Our conversation moves on to mushrooms, as this is the season and I tell him I have seen some but not picked them because I do not know which are poisonous and which are not. He tells me about the young boy who was out picking mushrooms one day about five or six years ago not far from here. He apparently put his hand in the wrong place and was bitten by a viper.

'He ran for help, which was very bad. Running increases the circulation and helps the poison go through the blood system. He was found dead.'

Do I just sit and hope that help will somehow miraculously appear? Or do I hurry for aid and drop dead before I can find it?

In my first week, the neighbours advised wearing shoes all the time outside — there were reports that a dog had been bitten and killed by a viper, so I should give myself some chance of avoiding the fangs by wearing protection on my feet. They actually didn't need to tell me that, because even the ground you walk on attacks you. Tough chicory plants with roots more than 30 cm deep infest the lawn, leaving sharp, stubby stems at ground level when you cut the grass. You would not be able to walk more than a foot or two on my lawns without suffering deep puncture wounds across your soles. Then there are the thistles that also lie in treacherous wait. After these come the grass burrs that cling to your socks and gradually insinuate themselves through the wool to gouge and dig into your skin.

And let's not forget the trees and shrubs . . . acacias with vicious barbs almost three centimetres long that can shred leather, let alone your skin; pretty shrubs with very unpretty thorns that can do the same; there are blackberries and brambles; nettles set your skin on fire.

It seems every plant growing here is designed to intimidate, or more nastily, penetrate the skin of the hapless humans who dare to invade their realm.

This is a dangerous world I have made my home. It is also one that can really bug you — literally. There is a huge array of bugs, insects, creepy crawlies and other sundry small treasures of the animal world to distract, annoy and harass you.

There are midges that incinerate themselves on the lamp above my kitchen bench. Their black corpses littering the gleaming white surface each morning puts me in mind of the Somme after yet another futile attack.

There are spiders and daddy-longlegs that set up elaborate cobweb systems in the highest reaches of my vaulted ceilings. One even found its way into my jeans on the washing line.

There are moths that immolate themselves on the halogen light bulb at the bottom of my stairwell. The smell as they sizzle in the incandescent heat is terrifyingly similar to the smoke of a burning house.

There are lizards and geckos by the hundreds in cracks in the walls, under stones, in the ground. They scuttle and slither if you make a noise or get too near. If you are not aware of them near you, they can give you quite a scare as they scuttle away over a bit of tin.

There are bugs that you don't hear until they suddenly plummet to the floor, making a loud crash as they hit the tiles.

There are mosquitoes that attack in the middle of a summer's night without warning. I am used to New Zealand mosquitoes that will hover within ear range, droning annoyingly for what seems an hour before launching their attack on your flesh. But these Italian mosquitoes are like their namesake from World War II — swift fighter planes that attack without warning and land on your skin with a very distinct thud. Insect repellent does little to deter them and, in the heat of a summer's night, you find yourself encased by your bedding with just a nose poking out to allow you to survive until morning.

Then there is the wood worm. While not posing an immediate danger to one's health, they do attack the massive beams that are needed to prop up the heavy terracotta tiled roofs. In abandoned farmhouses and sheds, these beams can suddenly give way, weakened by the last wood worm that broke the beam's back. Heavy timbers and the tiles they have been supporting come crashing to the floor. I stay well clear of these places.

The very ground itself poses a threat. This part of the world is earthquake territory. In my first few weeks here, a large earth tremor laid waste to the historic town of Assisi and the region around it. A second jolt later in the day killed two Franciscan friars and an art restoration expert inside the basilica of St Francis of Assisi, inspecting damage to 13th and 14th century frescoes badly damaged by the first one. Assisi is just 80 kilometres from San Clemente. In fact I felt the first quake, but not the second.

Fortunately, I am accustomed to these massive shifts of the

earth's crusts as my home in New Zealand was very close to a major fault line and earthquakes were quite common. I look forward to the first time Nancy feels an earthquake. 'Oh, that,' I shall say with a smug, serene air. 'Just an earthquake. Get those all the time back in New Zealand.' Let's see how she reacts to that!

As if all this was not enough to worry about, I also have had to be on my guard from my fellow human beings. I have already noted that autumn is the beginning of the hunting season. How excitable are these hunters if they see anything — and by anything I mean me — move? Will they shoot first and ask questions later?

Then there is the Italian Air Force.

Every now and then, they play cowboys and Indians over Trequanda and San Clemente, dog-fighting and chasing each other over the hills and valleys and ridges. They roar across the sky barely 300 metres above the villa. One morning, a jet fighter broke through the sound barrier and sent a cascade of crashing sound booming around *sotto i monti*. I have a number of fears about these Tom Cruise lookalikes. If they miscalculate their swoops and dives and banks, which house will they crash into? If they carry even dummy rockets or bombs, will they release one by mistake in their obvious excitement? If so, can I expect some such object to come plummeting through my roof or into my garden while I am underneath it, much like those vivid video clips from Operation Desert Storm where we saw some object hurtle down a chimney and then the entire building explode outwards?

All this I discovered in my first six weeks in Tuscany. What perils and dangers would lie in ambush for me in the coming seasons, I wondered.

And as the months rolled by I was to be constantly reminded that this is, indeed, a place where nature is a cruel mistress, where death is as much a part of life as life itself. Vignettes spring to mind. A still-living green lizard in the fanged kiss of a grass snake, its face raised to the sky with stoic acceptance of its grisly fate. Two wasps trying to sting each other to death on the lawn beneath the tree laden with ripe plums in early summer. Smoke as if from a burning cigarette butt drifting in the late afternoon sun that was, in fact, dust from a moth's wings being dislodged into the air as its body was devoured by a lizard.

For all its beauty, San Clemente is a place of violence, of imminent life and sudden death.

CHAPTER NINE

Passion and Perfume

IN THE THREE short weeks between Nancy's first and second visit to San Clemente our relationship grew through letters and telephone calls. For my part, the letters also reflected the despair of the separation and isolation that I was feeling. The idea of her taking an extended leave of absence to come to Italy for two or three years had run up against her company's policy of allowing only a month's leave at a time, with extensions by request at the end of each month. Once again we were back to square one. Should she apply for a transfer to another of the company's locations at the end of her project in Bath at the end of the following June? Or should she return to corporate headquarters in the United States, a prospect she did not relish if other options were available. If she went back to America I would have to join her there.

Then came a telephone call with some startling news. Visitors from corporate headquarters had arrived in Bath and announced that they wanted her to return immediately to New

Jersey. When was the soonest she could leave?

An hour later they had gone and Nancy's life was in turmoil.

'So how would you feel if I left here and came to live with you?'

My heart raced at the prospect. 'But what about your career?'

'I don't have a career. I'm never going to get any further because I don't play office politics.'

She was also tired of the ten- and twelve-hour days, the commuting, the unrelenting demands of the American corporate environment.

'I almost got out three years ago but I didn't. Now I have this opportunity.'

We would discuss this when she came on her second visit, but she was almost totally convinced this is what she would do.

Her vacation in Italy was not affected; she was owed holiday time and her flight had already been booked. She had her tax situation to organise and she would quietly put her house on the market so that she was ready to move as soon as the other arrangements were in place. I asked if it was wise to sell her house and car. But she did not want to go back to New Jersey anyway, and a house would be a financial and physical burden while she was here — if she came.

So this is what we would discuss as the last weeks of autumn died like the golden leaves of the woods and fields. After twenty years in the demanding and selfish world of multinational America, she would, I hope, find peace and tranquillity in San Clemente.

And new sensations . . .

. . . Buyer and seller alike were studying the small display of produce between them with close attention. In the gloom of the 700-year-old castle, they discussed the purchaser's exact requirements and then began carefully sifting through the possibilities, no more than 50 items at most. It seemed as if some ancient arcane rite was taking place. And, in its way, it was.

First, the seller would consider a selection then extract one of the small, mud-grey objects from the pile. He would turn it around in the light of the lamp overhead, assessing its merits and its suitability for the client opposite, who would also examine it with concentration.

The two would then discuss the sample, pointing to its size, discussing any skin blemishes, considering its potential for pleasure.

Sometimes the sample would be returned to the pile with a fatalistic shrug of the shoulders; sometimes it would be handed to a 'second' behind the seller for weighing and pricing. It was a labour of love, a careful, caring and even tender process in which both parties appreciated the need to match the right product to the right buyer.

The produce receiving so much attention is the stuff of culinary lore, legend and myth, prized for its powers to perfume and flavour the humblest pasta, the tenderest steak or the choicest cheese. And yet this careful ritual was not just because of its rarity, nor because the price value placed on this dour, dusty, nuggety item made customer satisfaction essential. I thought the tag on the table by the small pile was miswritten. 'Per kilogram?' I asked the salesman, pointing to the 320,000 lire figure. 'Hectagram,' he said. 'Cento grammi [100 grams],' I asked, wanting to make sure. 'Si. Three milioni otto cento lire per kilogram.'

When I let out a whistle of disbelief — a quick calculation showed the price at some $US2000 a kilo — he smiled and shrugged as if to say, 'That's what the market will pay. At Alba [another important truffle centre, to the north], cinque milioni

[5,000,000] lire.' He was letting me know the price was a bargain.

Here in the ancient hilltop town of San Giovanni d'Asso, just 20 kilometres from San Clemente, it is the last day of the annual celebration of *tartufo bianco* — the white truffle. The truffle is regarded with as much mysticism and reverence as were the pagan gods of the Etruscans who built rural settlements here as much as ten centuries ago.

This is the occasion for gourmands to show how seriously they take this object that arouses so much passion and reverence in the great restaurants of the world.

We are in the centre of Le Crete, the dramatic, barren landscape that both excites the eye and disturbs the mind. And this is where the autumn harvest of the white truffle takes place in the woods and riverbanks.

For two weekends in November, this little town on the road between Siena and Montalcino becomes a mecca for truffle lovers. They come by car from Florence and Rome and Milan. They come by train from Siena and Grosseto, on central Italy's western coast. And, like Nancy and myself, they come from the towns and villages surrounding San Giovanni d'Asso for the 12th annual Mercato Tartufo Bianco delle Crete Senesi, the trade show and festival celebrating the white truffles of Le Crete.

They come to learn the history of the truffle, to see the photographic displays, to taste the rare flavour it has to offer the palate, to discover the areas where these nodule-like members of the funghus family are to be found, to purchase other famed products of this rich region — the highly-prized extra-virgin oil known as Podere (and this is the season of the olive harvest and pressing as well), the ewe's milk cheese or pecorino which can be bought in three stages of ripening, the rich beef of the white cattle known as Chianina . . .

And perhaps they may also buy a small nugget of white truffle to take home and savour. For here they can purchase truffles at a bargain basement price because the stalls at this festival do not have to impose the high sales tax that shops and markets must apply. In Italy, a luxury item like *tartufo bianco* attracts a hefty 49 per cent.

Nancy and I join a privileged group of media, security personal, officials and spin doctors who sit down in a large room in the local elementary school to experience a meal that will linger long on the palate and in the memory. It is a feast dedicated to demonstrating the potency of this fruit of the chalk clay. We are also celebrating the culinary power of that other highly-prized and highly-priced cooking ingredient, saffron. This is because local officials are trying to encourage farmers to try producing these deep, glowing gold filaments from the autumn crocus — three hair-like, centimetre-long filaments per flower.

It is thus a rich repast indeed that we share — in both senses of the word.

This is our meal:

Trippa bianco allo zafferano (white tripe with saffron)
Gnocchi di patate al tartufo bianco (small boiled potato balls with white truffles)
Risotto allo zafferano (risotto-style rice with saffron)
Girello di chainina arrosto tartufo (slices of roast Chianina beef with a rich truffle gravy)
Pecorino delle Crete Senesi (pecorino cheese impregnated with tiny truffle slivers)

To help us wash this down, we are treated to a selection of fine wines this region is also famed for — Bianco Vergine di Valdichiana, Vino Nobile di Montepulciano and Moscadello di Montalcino.

'With truffles?' cheekily asks the vibrant young Frenchwoman at our table as our last course, a trifle-like *zuppa inglese al vin santo*, is placed before us. But she has no malice, just a great sense of humour that has amused and entertained us throughout our meal.

For the unfortunate souls beyond our four walls who are denied our luxuries, there are ample opportunities to indulge their taste for white truffles. A large marquee in the small paved area at the entrance to the castle is in full swing offering samples or complete meals. The bars and cafés of the town's one main street have barbecues or tables set up outside. The Tonino restaurant further up the High Street is promoting a special fixed price menu featuring a variety of courses involving truffles (price: 55,000 lire a head).

That seems a reasonable deal when one reads the 100,000 lire bill for a similar, truffle-celebrating menu at La Torre, the restaurant at the abbey of Monte Olivetto Maggiore, some dozen or so kilometres towards Siena.

So we remain quite content, thank you, to share the hospitality of our hosts at this table in San Giovanni d'Asso. We are, indeed, a mixed bag. There is the other Nancy, a large American woman who has lived in the historic town of Cortona for some 20 years. She is a food and wine writer and is here for the *New York Times*. Her companion John is on holiday; the bed-and-breakfast/restaurant he runs in a seaside town in Maine is closed for the winter.

Then there is our French entertainer, a charming girl from Amiens who works for the French food and wine trade promotion board and who was posted to Rome just three months ago. Her boyfriend is also from Amiens. He is a house painter and looking for work. Also seated with us is one of our Italian hosts involved in the publicity and promotion of the festival. And of course there is myself, the Kiwi, and my own Nancy from New Jersey.

During the meal we discover some background about the truffles. The person said to have discovered truffles was a French peasant, Joseph Talon, who somehow stumbled across them in oakwoods grown from acorns in a natural truffle-producing area. Rightly convinced he had become the owner of a precious secret, he kept the location of his bounty hidden and became a rich man until envious relatives spied on him and spread the news. Even today, truffle hunters jealously guard their secret sites, much the same as porcini mushroom gatherers protect their favourite 'patches'.

The truffles develop in symbiosis with certain trees like oaks and willows, the spores growing on their roots. More importantly, they can only thrive in environmental conditions that suit them. Factors like soil, water, minerals and temperature have to be in harmony, hence the truffle's rarity.

From the castle ramparts you can look down onto the small valley below. In the distance is a line of willow trees along a small stream. That is where the local truffle collectors go in search of this unprepossessing-looking delicacy.

In more modern times, mass communication through newspaper, magazines and television created a gold rush mentality. Landowners and simple sharks began to sell off patches of land they claimed was ideal for truffle growth, using names of spurious 'scholars' to support their promises of riches from beneath the soil. To counter this, and protect the genuine collectors and landowners, laws were introduced to control their harvesting. In Italy, collectors must be tested before being given an official licence. (The cynical might claim that in highly taxed, bureaucratic Italy this is merely another revenue-gathering scheme.) Some landowners set up co-operatives to control truffle-hunting on their acreage. Non-members face arrest if they are found gathering truffles illicitly on this land.

Because the funghi grow beneath the surface of the land, the collectors need help to find them. Traditionally, pigs were used to sniff them out because they love to eat them. Nowadays, in Italy, mixed-breed dogs have replaced pigs as the collector's primary hunting tool.

It takes time and money to train the dogs, which are less interested in truffles than the pigs. The first step is to convince the dog to retrieve a rubber ball. Then, a piece of ripe gorgonzola cheese replaces the ball. When the dog learns to 'fetch' it, the cheese is hidden. A truffle then replaces the cheese and, finally, is buried for the dog to uncover.

Not surprisingly, truffle dogs become valuable animals, worth thousands of dollars. They are also the targets of their owners' truffle-hunting competitors. During my first truffle season, a vicious war broke out in Umbria, one of Tuscany's adjacent provinces where truffles are also found. More than 30 dogs were killed by strychnine poisoning. Such is the passion for and value of the truffle.

Today, about a third of truffles gathered each year come from cultivation. Young trees are greenhouse grown, their roots steeped in a broth containing truffle spores. They are then planted in the same area where truffles are found naturally in the wild. At San Giovanni d'Asso, for example, there is an extensive planting of these greenhouse trees around the existing wild truffle site.

We also learn that you never cook truffles.

'No, no, no. Never,' exclaims our French lady. Nancy of the *New York Times* agrees.

'Cooking takes away all their flavour. First you cook your course and then just before serving you add the truffles,' she says, demonstrating a grating motion over her plate.

From the food we have had, it is clear that only the smallest shavings are needed — a reflection of their high flavour and equally high price tag. For the really serious truffle eater, there are special grating implements available to produce the fine particles that are sprinkled over the meal. There are various truffle additives available that allow the common man to sample the taste — oils, salsas and sauces, with the truffles generally mixed with porcini.

But for the true connoisseur, only the real thing will do — if you can afford it.

CHAPTER TEN

The Mezzadria

AN EERIE, SILENT ghost town lies scattered about the hills and ridges of San Clemente. It is a landscape littered with dead houses, inhabited, it seems, by ghosts from a centuries-old tradition, the *mezzadria*. This was the system of sharecropping that was the farming way of life here for some six centuries. Yet in just a few short years after World War II, the ancient co-operative contract between peasant and landowner became extinct.

The collapsing shells of homes where peasant families lived above their livestock and their livelihood are all that remain — haunting reminders of how swift and complete the advance of progress has been as it hurtles into the new millennium. Some, like San Clemente, have been resurrected by new city money that has flowed back to the countryside. These are now beautifully rustic vacationers' hideaways, or the homes of wealthy expatriates (*stranieri*) lured to the magic of the Tuscan environment. But many of these stark, abandoned symbols of the *mezzadria* remain, decaying under the twin assault of climate and neglect.

Their collapse has been slower than the system that created them, perhaps a testament to the strength of their construction and the care of the peasants whose lives were inextricably linked to them philosophically, financially and emotionally. Now they are a silent and dangerous world to enter. Half-metre square roof beams are eaten away by wood worms, floors can suddenly snap under the weight of their tiles, vipers can make their homes in the rubble left behind.

Two of these gaunt skeletons rot on the lane down to San Clemente. The first is Casa Nova, with a beautiful colonnade of arched openings onto an outside veranda, matched by similar arched openings for the animal stalls below. On summer days when the Chianina cattle are grazing in the field it overlooks, the bleached-white animals will seek shelter from the sun in these former stalls. It seems so wonderfully ironic. The lane now turns sharply at Casa Nova, dividing the house from the former outbuilding that may have perhaps once housed pigs or chickens. One day in early spring when the snow still lay heavily on the ground and buildings, I noticed its weight had collapsed the roof of the outbuilding overnight — a sharp reminder of how dangerous these once-proud farm buildings have become.

Further down the lane lies Poggio Felice (Happy Hill), another grand old farmhouse with a wide central set of steps leading to its rotting front door. Inside, many of its upstairs floors have collapsed and in one room the tiles sink precariously earthward. It is no place to venture safely.

From the back lawn of San Clemente, as I sit with wine and salad in the sun, I can see them clearly, glowing golden in the light. Their long-gone doors and windows gape blackly, like decayed or missing teeth in the smile of a lost era. Even San

Clemente carries a reminder of this extinct life. Across the narrow enclosed courtyard from the main house stands the remains of a former outbuilding. The roof has given way with neglect, a pile of old beams now riddled and rotten with worms all that remains. One section of roof still shelters a former animal stall, but its beams need supports to keep it in place. It could collapse at any time and I am wary about going in there. The walls that remain have large cracks, also threatening to succumb to old age, to give up and die like the *mezzadria*. These relics of the past, at least those not revived by modern wealth, seem then like death itself.

In my first year in Tuscany I learned about the *mezzadria*, how it arose, how it worked, and how it collapsed. And I was fortunate enough to have it brought richly and colourfully back to life the way it existed at San Clemente.

The beginnings of the *mezzadria* date back eight centuries to when the feudal system of great estates broke up. The owners — landless, serfless and, in many cases, penniless — moved to the cities, to lick and heal their economic wounds and pride. The hapless serfs followed their former owners to such famed towns and cities as Siena, Florence, Arezzo and Perugia, where population and trade offered survival. The new environment required new skills and this migrant population learned to master trades like baking or ironmongery or leather working. With skill and time came wealth. But the love of the land remained in their blood and, like their 20th century counterparts, these *nouveau riche* began reinvesting in their heritage, buying up the land their grandparents or older ancestors had deserted.

But life — and money — was good in the city, so the reborn landowners hired contractors to work the land for them. It was a simple but elegant system that provided for both parties. The landowner would pay for seed, equipment and maintenance of

Above: *The villa San Clemente with old Sinalunga in the distance.*

Below: *Trequanda's main square, Piazza Garibaldi.*

Above left: *The beauty of Tuscany.* Above right: *A typical street scene in Pienza.*

Below left: *A hardware shop in Pienza.* Below right: *Street scene in Montepulciano.*

Right: *Nancy in Siena's famous piazza, Il Campo.*

Below: *Lunchtime at the vendemmia.*

Above left: *Nancy and the foot bath at Bagno Vignoni.*
Above right: *Elario at the olive harvest.*

Below left: *Allan and harvest time at San Clemente.* Below right: *White truffle festival of San Giovanni d'Asso.*

the farm while the *mezzadro*, or contract labourer (in effect, a peasant) would do the donkey work of ploughing, sowing, reaping and generally running the farm. The economic basis was equally simple — a 50:50 split of any profits or, in bad years, losses.

To the modern, city-raised mind it seems an idyllic lifestyle, raising food and family in the hills of southern Tuscany. The reality was anything but. It was a desperate, back-breaking life, forever dependent on the weather and the number of hands available to do the dawn-to-dusk work. Large families were required to provide labour to till the fields, tend the animals, fetch the water, pick the fruit — the countless chores needed to run an all-purpose farm without the latter-day luxury of tractor, harvester, hay-baler and water pump. And all for just 50 per cent of the profits — or, worse, the losses that would have to be repaid in the good years.

A harsh life, indeed. But for 500 years it worked. It carried a sense of justice and rightness that commanded, for the most part, respect from both parties to this social and economic contract. As Tuscan economist Jacopo Mazzei wrote in *Firenze furale*, the system survived on the 'conviction of fairness'. He forecast — rightly — that it would die when this conviction turned to scepticism and mistrust between the two parties. And so it happened, through the very economic system that was purportedly created to enrich and ennoble the lives of the poverty-stricken, slave-like working masses of the world.

The irony is both rich and sad. Communism became — and remains — a strong and well accepted political force in Tuscany. Communist partisans were actively involved in the underground war against the Fascists of Hitler and Mussolini. Their siren song to the poor, slavish *mezzadro* drew him with its sweet promise of a higher profit-sharing percentage and, later, the prospect of his own land — taken from the 'greedy' landowner and split into small holdings for families. In the aftermath of the destruction of the war, this was an emotive and heady temptation and resentment grew swiftly between farm owner and tenant. The *mezzadria*'s half-and-half system became more favourable to the peasant. The disgruntled landowners, their profit margin cut, would or could no longer fund the essentials needed to keep their farms operational. And the peasant families certainly did not have the money to do so. Those 'lucky' enough to get a smallholding of their own were faced with a desperate and in most cases insurmountable need to provide an infrastructure to support their new-found independence — roads needed to be built, woodland cleared, swamps drained. Economic independence from the 'ownership' of the absentee landlord was a myth.

At the same time, better education and the lure of the city lights were also breaking down the *mezzadro*'s family itself — the foundation on which the entire system had been based for all those centuries. Young wives were no longer happy to be part of a society where mother-in-law ruled supreme. And the peasant's children were not content with the back-breaking toil needed; a better-paid, easier and less arduous job in town seemed a much more attractive proposition. Who can blame them?

So within a decade or so in that post-war era, the *mezzadria* vanished. The landowner remained in his distant city. The young people escaped to the town and, without the labour or money to continue, the peasant and his wife retired to the local village. One estimate suggests some 600,000 Tuscan peasants left their land in the 1950s. All that remains to remind later generations of the years of the *mezzadria* are the abandoned homes and farm buildings, dying as slowly but as surely as the people who once filled them with so much life.

❧

One afternoon during my first year, this ancient way of life was amazingly and colourfully reborn. For just a few fascinating hours I was to glimpse how things were for a *mezzadro* family at San Clemente.

When I first saw Elario Mancini he was picking the olives in my neighbour Airdrie's small grove. I had wanted to ask him about the olive-pressing and to see if he could help me go there. Ever obliging and helpful, he was able to do that and the result is recounted in Chapter 7.

As we talked on that late November morning, he told me he had been raised as a child at San Clemente when his family lived there under the *mezzadria* system. This was too good to be true, particularly as his years here included the German occupation of San Clemente in the war and the subsequent fighting that took place. He was a living history book and I was eager to read from his memories.

I had prepared for his visit in advance with questions and my trusty cassette recorder to catch his every word. My preparations were, as it turned out, a futile exercise as Elario simply began touring the grounds and the house, reliving his youth and pointing out the special places of that time. He arrived with his new bride, Eva, a delightful Polish woman, and a bottle of wine from his own grapes, unlabelled and freshly-capped (not corked) that morning. 'Is natural wine. No chemicals, only grapes from last year,' he told me. It was to prove a charming wine, light and not mouth-puckeringly dry. I had arranged to pick him up at the top of the lane to spare his car the roughness of the road surface down to the villa. Even before we reached San Clemente, he was recalling how it had been.

'There was a bridge over here,' he said, pointing to the place where a small stream bed now flows through a culvert under the metalled road. 'We used to scare each other at night coming back from Poggio Felice or Casa Nova playing cards. We would hide under there and pretend we were awful scary monsters.' At the sharp bend in the road just before reaching the villa, he pointed to the ploughed field. 'There we had a vineyard. Very, very good wines. Very strong. It was good land, very rocky.' Pointing to the field on the other side of the house, he said: 'Vines there also but not so good, not many rocks.' And gesturing to the field on the other side of the road: 'There were the olives and the peaches and the almonds. Beautiful, beautiful peaches.'

Elario was lost, back in his boyhood. But it was a journey through time that I was privileged to join for two hours. It was the first time since 1952 that he had come back to the home of his childhood. Today he lives in the little neighbouring town of Castelmuzio. It was there that I helped sack the olive harvest to take to press.

As we pulled up outside the front entrance, he pointed to the big acacia tree. 'I planted that. It was very small,' he said, lowering his hand to knee height. Now it stands some fifteen metres high, and overshadows smaller acacias that have grown from its fallen seeds. In its prime, he said, it had 'very good fruit' although it had borne none in my first year. Every tree he planted, it seemed, produced a wonderful crop. Some still do — the figs that are so delicious to pluck and eat, for example — but many have disappeared, through disease, the needs of modern farming or just old age. Like the *mezzadria* itself they were an anachronism, a memory only from that vanished past when living off the land was vital for survival, a past when there were no hypermarkets and no money to spare on store-bought foodstuffs. As we walked around the property, more places of former trees were identified. There, by the compost heap, was a 'very good' apple tree he planted, now gone. We walked down the lane to find a pear tree. Gone, too, like its counterparts in the field. As was the big mulberry tree at the entrance to the drive from the lane. 'Wedding parties walking up to the Abbadia Sicile [the old abbey still visible on the skyline from San Clemente] from Arezzo, or Sinalunga or Perugia would stop to have a picnic under there.'

In winter, people would come up to *i monti* from the valley floor when it was foggy on the flat. They brought their laundry to dry in the sun higher up, driving up with their two-wheel carts drawn by a bull. The journey up would take half a day. They would hang out their washing, have lunch, then pack up for the journey back down.

One ancient, gnarled mulberry still stands at San Clemente, between the bountiful plum tree and the acacia that Elario planted as a seedling. The heart of its trunk has rotted away, leaving a big empty cave. Its only purpose in life now, it seems, is to stain white laundry with light-mustard spots as its sickly-sweet fruit drops on the clothesline beneath its limbs in summer. I quickly learned to hang only dark clothes underneath it.

And so our tour continued. My questions and tape recorder lay on the kitchen table as I trailed behind his excited footsteps, like the dust cloud behind our jeep as we come down the dirt lane in summer. 'I loved trees but no one else in my family interested,' he said. But they certainly reaped the bounty of his interest — fresh figs in late summer and autumn or dried in the cold months, pears and apples, berries and nuts.

'We never buy anything from the shop, maybe sardine or dry fish sometime. But we have never been hungry. We were always eating plenty.' He recalled the omelettes his mother made from the fresh chicken eggs, the funghi, the figs and grapes dried and stored in an alcove above the wood beside the fireplace upstairs. A special treat each year were the two capons — *caponi de lia* — that the family feasted on.

Meat was a rare treat, a small morsel perhaps once a week. For important feast days like Christmas or Easter the family might kill a pig. From it they would get roasts, chops, prosciutto, salami . . . even the blood was put to use as black sausage.

'We throw away nothing.'

Most of the produce was sold to buy staples.

'Every Tuesday, the women walked to Sinalunga market to sell a few rabbits, chickens or pigeons. Use the money for buying salt, sugar . . .'

Today, the people still flock to the Tuesday Sinalunga market, as we do, albeit with the benefit of motorised transport rather that foot power.

Walking was the only way to get around. Each morning, Elario and his brothers and sisters would walk through the fields to school at Trequanda.

'No cars, no buses, no tractors . . .'

His interest in growing things extended beyond fruit trees. He rediscovered the small succulents that he 'planted' on the tile roof above the back outbuilding shed that we now use for storing gardening equipment. He had brought a few little plants back from an outing to Arezzo. Now they cover most of the remaining roof tiles and spill over the edge. My fledgling garden was to go against the wall there, beneath the overhanging plants, where it would get the afternoon sun. In Elario's childhood, he said, two small sheds — 'for the chickens and for the milk' — stood where our first garden was laid. But today there is no sign of them. A little further out, the family had its winter garden; the summer garden was on the other side of the house, now in lawn. The family pigs were housed in two sheds on the same side as the summer garden. At least some remnants of these remain — the brick walls. But they stand roofless and covered with ivy.

The two cattle ponds that lie in the fields on either side of the house held special memories for Elario. The furthest one was an oasis for summer fruit and vegetables. 'We used to grow tomatoes, watermelons . . . very beautiful.' The other, the one overseen from the kitchen window, was the scene of a family tragedy when Elario's brother, only six years old, fell in one night and drowned. And so the Mancini family dropped in numbers from twelve (seven sisters and five sons) to eleven.

The pond was also another good source of food and free entertainment. As children, the kids would sit by its side, waiting to skewer members of the very vocal frog population with home-made, primitive devices. 'We had long sticks to go over the water. At the end was a flat board with a nail going through it. When a frog came to the surface, we would strike down, catching it with the nail. Oh yes, we ate them — very good, too.' The frogs still croak in the pond at nights and hang, limbs outstretched, on the surface or on the banks when the weather is warm.

Sparrows too, were a useful food source. Attracted to the grain from the harvest, they would come by day to the back courtyard and its sheds. At roosting time, they would return to their trees, flying through a gauntlet of sacks the family laid from the top corner of the house where the birds flew out. 'We would get 40 or 50 in an afternoon. Very small but very delicious.'

Less pleasant were Elario's memories of the work the whole family was expected to do to survive in the beautiful but demanding, even primitive, environment of the *mezzadria*.

'All year long working on the farm — maize, potatoes, grapes, olive trees, grain . . . never have holiday. When I am nine years I started to work on the farm. We go to school in Trequanda in morning and work in afternoon, looking after pigs and sheep. That was the children's work.' But there was much more — drawing water from the deep-sunken tank, filled by rain run-off from the roof, with a bucket attached to a rope and pulley. 'After an hour your hands are very, very sore.' In my first summer, drawing the water from the tank was to take on a special significance as I, too, was forced to use the well *a la mezzadria*. Another water supply, in the same field as the frog pond but no longer there, was a source of 'very, very good water' that the children collected in barrels and brought back to the house on a horse- or cow-driven cart. Flippantly, I wondered if one cow power is the same as one horsepower.

'It was very, very hard work here, specially in summer. In summer we make [fire] wood in the forest. In spring there are other jobs — digging, cleaning . . .'

In summer the men and the boys would be up at first light to cut and collect grain and hay from the fields.

'Sometimes up at 3 am, sometimes finish at 12 at night. Use sickle to cut grain and then carry it home. Nowadays, there are machines,' he said wistfully.

Every two or three weeks, the gathered grain would be taken to the village to be made into flour.

And there was never much money for treats. 'You were only half owner so only little money. When you sell pigs or lambs or cheeses, money would stay in *conto* (the farmer's bank account) in Trequanda. You never see it.' For this was the way of the *mezzadria* — farm income was 'pooled' for the purchase of seed, equipment, and maintenance with the rest split between Elario's family and the owner.

But the family had its ruses.

'Every day my mother make cheese. Supposed to be one cheese for us and one for owner.' Once a month, a man would come from Trequanda to collect the cheeses, and other produce from the farm, taking 50 per cent.

'But always we pinch something.'

His mother, he said, would always make two equal rounds of cheese for the share system. But she would also make an extra half-sized round.

'We keep the small one.'

The relentless battle for survival meant Christmas was a meagre one at San Clemente.

'Never have Christmas tree. No farmers had Christmas trees — trees all around in woods so no need. Villages and towns yes, but not farm. On Christmas Eve we get a stocking with little treats like caramels. But no presents, no clothes, no shoes, nothing like that.'

In Elario's time at San Clemente, the farm waved up and down some 80 hectares of the land that surrounds me. The owner of all this land was, and remains, the pension fund of the Banco Lombardi de Milano. Of San Clemente's history, Elario sadly knew little, not even its age. But he was able to give me the fascinating detail of how it came to be a bank-owned property. 'At one time there were two *conti* [counts] living in Trequanda, one on this side of the town and one on the other side. The one on this side owned 42 farms but lost them all to the other at cards. The winner went to Monte Carlo and lost everything, so the land went to the *banco*. After the war, the owner became the Fundo Pension, but the bank still own it.' And engraved on a concrete plaque on a wall at the abandoned Casa Nova we can still just read the weather-beaten lettering, Fundo Pension. Underneath the house title and ownership announcement there is another inscription on the plaque. But it has been chiselled out and now resembles chicken scratchings. A similar plaque is attached to one of the walls at San Clemente, with the name of the *casa* and, again, those chicken scratchings. I had thought the age of the house was inscribed there, but was puzzled why it would be chiselled away. Elario was able to enlighten me, even if not to the age of the house.

When Mussolini and his Fascist Party came to power, it became very wise for Italians to proclaim their support for the new government. So even in such a left-leaning area as southern

Tuscany, plaques announcing support for Fascismo, engraved into concrete as solid proof of this new-found enthusiasm, were quickly erected onto the walls of buildings. Stone masons and concreters must have had a field day. 'But after Mussolini dead, to have sign supporting Fascismo not so very good,' said Elario. So the concrete messages of goodwill and support were quickly chiselled away as they were on the plaque commemorating the 1932 arrival of water reticulation on the outside wall of Trequanda's modest town hall.

There were other dangers apart from the vengeful Communist partisans, such as the large wasp-like hornets that Elario made a special point of trying to kill. ('Very, very dangerous . . . eight, nine stings and you dead.')

'You see many snakes?' he asked as we came across a snake hole in the lawn.

'Yes, but no *vipore*,' I said. 'No, *vipore* live over there,' he pointed to the woods barely 150 metres from the house.

A large triangular-shaped stone sticking erect from the ground at the top of the drive took his attention. 'It should be there,' he said, pointing to the corner of the villa, two metres or so away from its current 'home' at the top of our short drive. 'There were stones like that on all corners of the house. They were there to stop the cart wheels hitting the house when it came in from the field.' And, yes, the stone was lined with indentations where countless cart wheel axles over countless years had jolted against it. The concept of this corner stone was remarkably simple and elegant in its practicality. It also had another practical use. The farm dogs would stop and have a pee against it as they passed, he explained, cocking his leg in an obvious demonstration. 'It was called *piscia cane*,' he added, using the Italian name that needed no translation. 'Sometimes still you call people you don't like that.' I wouldn't dare, I thought.

Then after one quick foray down the lane to show where the Mancini kids used to sit outside in the sun ('very nice place, sheltered from the north wind and very warm and sunny [it is now overgrown with the trees and vines of the woods]'), Elario was ready to go back into the home of his youth for the first time since 1956. 'When I come back from England, I come by here but nobody home,' he said. Any thoughts I had of leading him to my tape recorder and questions quickly vanished. Rather, it was Elario who led the guided tour of the life in a farmhouse in the *mezzadria*.

As we entered the large lobby, he pointed to the left where a glass-topped table adorned with a potted palm now stands. There the family's horse was used to cut hay and grass to a manageable size for the cows and bulls, round and round in a ceaseless circle. 'After three months, we don't need to work them. They go when in harness, we say stop, they stop. Chuck-a-chuck-a-chuck-a-chuck.' Around the corner, in a section of what is now the lounge, was the horse's stable. The rest of the lounge housed eight cattle. 'Here is where they were fed,' he said as he walked to the now closed-in, raised semi-wall against another wall, beside the grand piano and where the CD player and the music stands. 'In summer, the — what do you call them? — would fly around the roof because they could get in through the doors and open windows,' he said, extending out two fingers in a V shape. 'Swallows?' I suggested. 'Yes, swallows, that is them.'

The dining room, now resplendent with a twelve-seat formal glass-top table, was also a cattle stall, except for one small area against the wall to the kitchen. That was for the family's clutch of rabbits. The kitchen itself was originally where the herd of sheep were stalled. 'But they were moved out to there because they smelled so much,' said Elario, pointing to the outsheds through the now glassed back door. After their eviction, the room was used for making wine from the farm's vines.

The downstairs bathroom and separate toilet were storage areas for grains and animal feed. The little room beneath the stairs was for the chicken feed. Outside, across the narrow courtyard, more sheds and stalls were in use. At one end was the brick oven, still discernible with its ground-level fireplace opening (part of the foot-operated bellows still remain) and, above, the opening to the oven. Separate openings on either side of the oven led to more rabbit hutches.

'Here was a bench where my mother lined up the dough loaves to put in the oven,' Elario said, stretching his arms wide along a wall beside the oven for the bench. One hardy wooden support arm still juts from the wall.

'In winter, when the travelling people came walking by selling the jewellery and trinkets they would stay for the night. They always asked to sleep in the bread oven [above the ground-level fireplace]. It was very warm place to be.' That, I mused, was a very different angle on the old jokes about the travelling salesman and the farmer's daughter.

Our tour downstairs completed, we moved up to the former quarters where the 14-strong Mancini family lived and ate (later reduced by one, of course, with the death of Elario's brother). There are two bedrooms at the top of the landing. One was the boys' room — at least until Elario's older brother was married and took over the other for himself and his new bride. It had been a grain storage room until then. The library and Carlo's room were reserved for the seven sisters. Mother and father slept in what is now the main bedroom. 'There was only the one layer of tiles on the floor. When the cows made a noise, my father could lift up a loose tile to see what was happening below.'

The hub of the family was the lounge area, with its big fireplace where the food was cooked, the water was boiled and, in winter, the children sat around the raised hearth to keep warm. 'Was very good place to sit. Was very cold in winter when windows broken,' said Elario, wrapping his arms around himself and mock-shivering with his memories of those mist-shrouded, cold, bleak winter days. Beside the fireplace was an alcove for the firewood. Above it, the wooden mantel extending to the wall was used to dry fruits and other food.

In the centre of the room was the family table, where this large group ate, talked, planned the planting or harvest and played cards for entertainment. Cards seemed to be the major diversion in those days as Elario recounted stories of visiting Happy Hill, Casa Nova and Miciano for card evenings with the neighbours.

Other diversions included dance evenings at the farmers' homes around *i monti*. His brother would play the accordion at these evenings and Elario might organise the wine. In this way they earned a little money for themselves.

'But dancing only from September to February or March. Not in summer. Too tired from working in fields.'

'Did the fireplace smoke then?' I asked, mindful of attempts to set a fire only to be thwarted by clouds of smoke pouring back into the room.

'Oh yes, very bad smoke if the window is shut. Sitting at the table you would be coughing and your eyes were sore.' Why, after centuries of use, the various inhabitants had meekly continued to accept this foul-tempered, foul-smoking fireplace remains a mystery.

Elario was to escape the harsh life of the *mezzadria* when he was twenty-five. But in its own way, his new life was to have its hardships, at least in the early stages. His brother was offered a position in the London home of a wealthy pasta importer and manufacturer who was seeking a butler and cook. Elario's brother was not interested in moving to another country, let alone the mysteries of such a big foreign city.

'So I say to myself, why don't I go?'

In 1952, he and his wife arrived in London complete with a two-year contract and brand new passports. It was to be a rude arrival.

'We think it would be easy. But house had seven people and 31 rooms. We have to do all cooking, dishes, serving. After six months we become fed up.'

Tied to a contract, Elario turned to that eternal source of assistance, the British bobby. 'Police say, don't worry, we know this family. You go.'

Next the couple worked for a captain of the Queen's Guards.

'But after six months, they give him two soldiers to work for him.' The captain proved helpful, trying to secure a post with a decent family in London.

'He said if he no know name of family, job no good.'

Eventually a post was found in the home of the then Minister of Health.

'But she was mad, completely mad.' He explained that the woman insisted they do different work only at set times. 'From this time to this time, do this job. Then do that job.' Another employer, ironically an Italian lady in London — only paid him every six months. Finally, the Italian couple found a post with the English publisher George Weidenfeld, for whom he was to work for many years in London and, briefly, in New York. Later, after Elario returned to Italy, they were to continue exchanging Christmas cards.

In all, Elario lived abroad for 25 years. But he was able to return on holidays. These were an important way to smuggle saved money out of England to help his family.

Once, while working in a hamburger-patty factory ('I lose this there on machine,' he said, holding up a hand with a missing little finger) he used a cunning ruse to smuggle 2000

British pounds out of the country. At the time, it was illegal to export more than 200 pounds per year. He worked on a canning machine so one day brought in some sand and used it and the rolled-up notes to bring the can up to its proper weight. He then sealed the can and asked the factory manager if he could take the can of 'hamburger meat' to Italy for his family to taste. No problem, said the manager.

Another time, he cut out a square in a loaf of brown bread, scooped out the bread, stuffed the loaf with rolled-up ten-pound notes and glued the cut-out piece back.

'Was good. If Customs ask what's this, I say, "You no touch my bread."' He found fortune in other ways, too. After eighteen months in England, a friend he had made ('very old Russian woman, she spoke twelve languages') said he should play the football pools.

'I have never played before so she showed me. Later, a cheque arrived. I had never seen one before so I asked her what it was. She started jumping and screaming.' It was for 270 British pounds and two shillings — a fortune in those days.

Standing there with Elario, it was easy to imagine the scene all those years ago — a scene that had been continuous for so many centuries: the children keeping warm around the fireplace while a stew or soup simmered in a pot from the iron hooks still bedded into the bricks, perhaps some playing cards at the table where father planned the next day's activities, the room hazy with smoke from the burning oak logs hewed the last winter and dried during the hot summer . . . and the smell drifting up from the animal stalls below! Incredibly, this centuries-old scene was being played out less than 50 years ago.

At the time Elario left this home to live in England, I was six years old. We had a car, an electric stove and a washing machine. Jet aircraft flew over the Mancini farm. Computers were beginning to make their mark. Television was well established in the 'civilised' world. Yet here in the heart of rural Tuscany, a different life still flourished. It was a sobering thought, as was the realisation that even then it was already doomed, a last few years left before tradition lay prone before the demands and 'glamour' of a modern world.

CHAPTER ELEVEN

Nature's Palette: Rainbow Riches and Sotto la Nebia

IN MY FIRST autumn at San Clemente I became a man of many riches. As winter neared, the trees and plants in the woods that surrounded me turned to gold. It was an extraordinary sight. And the range of tonings was spectacular: butter gold, cinnamon gold, sunshine gold, tawny gold, coppery-gold, orange-tinted gold, bright yellow gold, dark yellow gold . . .

As I skirted the side of My Lady of the Mountains, the canopy of trees and her upward slopes gleamed so strongly in the autumn sunlight that they almost hurt the eyes. Even the very air seemed to have been washed with a golden tint. A golden parade of honour flanked me as I drove up and down my private road. The woods to the south and east shimmered in the sunlight. And the vines of the small wine estates between Trequanda and Sinalunga matched them for intensity.

Here and there were isolated highlights of different colours that served to emphasise the golden blanket that lay across my landscape. Leaves turned scarlet or crimson red, a rich brown that resembled the ploughed fields after the rains, bright oranges as intense as the mandarin-coloured citrus fruit and even the multi-hued greens of the defiant pines, firs and olives which resisted winter's call.

The cycle of harvest continued and the fields that were bare with the cropping, ploughing and replanting of my first weeks at San Clemente now became green with new life. The appearance above ground of the winter crop growth was a strong reminder of how rich and lush this land remains after so many millennia.

Then for ten days after my return from meeting Nancy's parents in New Jersey over Christmas, San Clemente was held prisoner by a damp, chill, white straitjacket. The mists advanced and retreated up the slopes, producing some extraordinary sights. From the top of my road, where it joins the road to Trequanda, I looked out over a vast white ocean with islands of hilly outcrops scattered sparsely across its surface. The mist that morning had crept up the valley slopes from the Valdichiana floor. Exhausted by its efforts, it stopped just below the level of the little knoll on which San Clemente sits. Away in the distance, only the old centre on the hilltop of Sinalunga was visible, another island in a sea that stretched the 40 or so kilometres across the Valdichiana to the next land mass — the distant Apennine mountain range.

Elsewhere I could see other islands rising from this endless sea. The mist was dense and bleached white. It was perfectly flat and level. And it stirred not one centimetre. Around me there was absolute stillness and quiet, as if the land and the air were reluctant to disturb this beautiful sea of white. This is how Jack must have felt as he reached the top of the beanstalk and his head broke through the clouds, with only the island castle of the giant in view.

At times during that big white-out through mid-January, the mist would enclose San Clemente and reach nearly to the top of my road. Ascending in the jeep, I would suddenly break through into blue sky and sunlight, with the wheels of the vehicle still shrouded in a white shawl. The sun seemed powerless to shift it. Perhaps it was building its reserves for the coming spring? For certainly, when a day dawned clear with a bright blue sky and an open view across the valley to the far hills, the sun had a real strength to warm the body and after so many days without it, the soul.

The long, lonely days and nights of winter at San Clemente had at times been desperate, relieved only by the reunion with Nancy at Christmas and again in February when she returned with friends Jean and Karen. But as spring poked a cautious nose into the air, the promise of new life revived my spirits. I was doubly reborn, both by the eternal cycle of nature and by the promise of my new life with Nancy as she prepared to move to Tuscany. It would be well into summer before she finally arrived and I would make two more visits to New Jersey. But in the meantime, there was a new season to discover at San Clemente.

There was the green, of course, as new leaves appeared on the trees, giving support to the silver-green of the stoical olive trees that had remained clothed through the winter. Then the sky began to grow on my lawn — the sky-blue little flowers of the chicory plants. Fields became dotted with blood as the crimson flowers of wild poppies blossomed. Bright red wild roses lined the path up my dirt road. Each day I was able to bring the sun inside San Clemente as I gathered daffodils from the roadside above the frog pond and the field in which it lay, now defrosted after its spring ice-melt. As the season advanced, the sun took over the land. Great fields of sunflowers — the symbol of the Tuscan landscape — blossomed into rich yellow.

Like soldiers on a parade ground they stood at silent attention in inch-perfect ranks, together facing their commander — the sun itself. They flowed up and down the rolling hillsides, great swathes of yellow stretching away into the distance.

As the flora emerged into the spring warmth, so too did the wildlife. Lizards came out of their winter nooks and crannies to scuttle through the grass and up the stone walls of the villa. The air became alive again with the buzz of flying insects. Ants' nests began appearing in the ground, their tell-tale little mounds of excavated earth producing a continuous trail of their inhabitants out hunting for food. The locals, too, seemed to emerge from winter dormancy as ploughing and sowing begin in the fields and I began to live under a rainbow that was to last right through the rest of my first year.

Summer just happened. It did not announce its arrival like a polite visitor, it simply drifted in unnoticed. One day I thought to myself, well, it's summer now.

At first there was the bride-white of the blackberry flowers; later, the white, then the Chianti red and finally the ebony of the fruit themselves. There was more white in my world, too, when the Chianina cattle were sent out to graze in the fields below the kitchen and along the side fence. The mauve of lavender plants lined the drive against the blue of the tiny blooms of the rosemary plants opposite.

My palette was dotted with earth colours. The rust of the newly ploughed soil, the breadcrust brown of freshly-mown hayfields that gradually turned to near-white as the mown grass dried, the brushed gold of the great rounds of baled hay as they glowed in the evening sun, casting long shadows and littering the fields like some scattered Stonehenge.

The animal and insect kingdom began a reign of noisy terror. Humming and buzzing filled the air. Crickets started up with a non-stop cacophony. The concerto from the frogs sunning themselves on the banks of their pond began early and loudly; they croaked on deep into the night. At least the grasshoppers were silent as they created a thigh-high bow wave before me when I walked across the lawn. Flies went swimming in my beer, gnats in the wineglass.

Above all, I remember the heat of that first summer. How many clichés apply? It was oppressive, stifling, furnace-like, blazing, burning, exhausting, oven-like, roasting, boiling . . .

I could only work outside until about 9.30 am each day before the heat drove me to the relative cool inside tile-floored San Clemente. Clothes fresh from the laundry would be almost dried by the time I finished pegging them on the line strung in the 'shade' between the plum and mulberry trees. Early afternoon was time for the siesta — but I could get a suntan lying on the bed as the afternoon sun sought me out through the window. Even the dumb cattle would seek shelter in the abandoned homes of the *mezzadria*. On a good day, a breeze might develop in the early afternoon. Mostly, however, it would be late afternoon before it arrived to cool the air enough to venture outside again.

CHAPTER TWELVE

Festivals and Fantasies

IT WAS LIKE Disneyland on acid. There was the mouse, but he had morphed into a leering, shark-toothed rodent whose eyes were the same blood red as the gore on the knife that stabbed up and down just inches from my face.

The wild-eyed, smoke-nostrilled bull had an equally gory stabbing sword in one hand and a bloody heart in the other. The fairy queen was a dyed-blonde harlot surrounded by a coterie of fanged monsters. Instead of the happy brass-band marching music of the Magic Kingdom, brain-bursting disco raged through the narrow cobbled streets.

Such was my initiation into carnival-time, Italian style.

The arrival of spring marks the beginning of festival season in Italy. From March until the end of the harvest in November, Italians come out to party, play and parade. The inhabitants of cities, towns and the tiniest of villages throw on their party costumes, face glitter and flags for a non-stop whirl of pageantry, competitions and historical recreations. Some celebrate the harvest — in the towns around me I can visit festivals and displays devoted to local produce from the land such as wine, olive oil, pecorino cheeses and white truffles. Others recognise the man-made products of the area, like the terracotta fair of Petroio. Montepulciano and Cortona host highly regarded jazz festivals. There are flower and sculpture festivals, medieval costume parades with jousting and crossbow contests. In neighbouring Montisi, for example, there is a festival each August commemorating a significant event which occurred in the town seven centuries ago.

In 1291, a member of the powerful Cacciaconti family who ruled this area demanded tribute from the town, said by some authorities to be named after the Etruscan goddess Isis whom they worshipped at a nearby temple. Facing resistance from the townsfolk, Simone Cacciaconti attacked the town. After a battle in which three of the defenders were killed, he destroyed it by fire, but not before plundering the villagers' possessions.

Today, on the Sunday nearest to 5 August (the feast day of the town patron, Our Lady of the Snows), the town stages the Giostra di Simone. 'Knights' representing the four *contrade*, or districts, of the town compete by charging 100 metres on horseback, wielding ferocious-looking iron-tipped lances at a wooden effigy of Simone. The effigy, the *buratto*, has a target disc and a ring called the *campanella* jutting from one shoulder. On the other is a *flagello*, a whip-like instrument with balls attached to wallop a hapless knight who is too slow in his attack. Each rider has four shots at lancing and carrying off the *campanella*, which is no wider than a small child's wrist bracelet. The rider with the most successes and thus points at the end earns glory for himself and a prized painted banner, *il panno*, for his *contrada*. It is an extraordinarily difficult feat.

While the riders take their turns galloping across the field, townsfolk clad in medieval costume or waving the flags of their particular *contrada* line the bank on the side of the field, cheering wildly when their representative scoops the ribboned ring onto his lance.

In Italy the honour of the *contrada* you live in is a serious business. Even the smallest village, like Montisi, has its separate *contrade*. Like a sports club, they have the 'team' colours, a flag with its own emblem, they record and respect their district's culture and history and they provide recreational activities. Each has its own patron or feast day. In previous centuries, *contrade* would form their men into distinct military groupings to send to wars against neighbours, much the same way as, say, battalions of soldiers were formed from English towns and cities during World War I. Today, mercifully, there is no longer a need to send the men of Tuscany or Lancashire 'over the top', but the deeds of the fighting forebears are remembered.

Perhaps the most famed manifestation of the *contrade* today is Il Palio, when flashing eyes, manes, whips and hooves turn Siena's Il Campo into a frenzy of excitement. This centuries-old horse race around the outer circumference of the piazza is contested between ten of the city's seventeen *contrade* with names like Aquila (Eagle: 'Of the eagle, the beak, the talon and the wing'), Pantera (Panther: 'The Panther roared and the people awoke') and Drago (Dragon: 'The ardour in my heart becomes flame in my mouth').

To understand the commitment to the *contrada* — its demands of love, loyalty, honour, and life-long devotion — is to understand the passion of the Italian heart.

My introduction to this way of life came in the small town of Foiano de Chiana on the first day of spring at the annual *Carnivale*. It was to be a surrealistic experience, a scene that Salvador Dali would have had difficulty conjuring even with his masterful imagination. This *Carnivale* did not begin until 1866; if it had been in existence a few centuries earlier, Dante might well have dropped by to use it as a setting for his *Inferno*. It was that kind of experience.

I had been invited to join a neighbour to drive the 30 or so kilometres to the festival. Foiano is a typical small town, standing on a hillock in the flat plain of the Valdichiana. As far as I could discern, its only feature of interest is the restaurant offering 'sex dinners' — a mélange of male and female strippers spread before you while you, presumably, enjoy your antipasto and ravioli. Perhaps the quality of the food is such that the proprietor feels he must divert your interest from it.

I had not known what to expect. Perhaps a medieval costume parade, perhaps some religious rite. But I was glad to accept the invitation to experience another slice of Italian life.

We arrived early, to get a carpark within reasonable walking distance of the town centre. Italians emerge for these affairs in great swarms, however banal the event, so we were keen to avoid a kilometre trek up the hill to the site. We decided to have a drink at a café in the tiny central piazza. Outside, we could see it slowly but surely filling with people as showtime neared. My companion went out to see what was happening. 'They're coming. It's fantastic,' she said as she came quickly back in to tell me.

'They' were the four fantastic floats of Foiano — a parade of gigantic papier-mâché caricatures of people, animals, demons and monsters. The four *contrade* of Foiano spend the year planning, designing and building these huge floats three stories high in a competition to be 'the best float in town'. They are designed to occupy most of the main street of the town where the parade takes place. Their creations are grotesque, surreal, phantasmagorical — luridly-coloured three-dimensional cartoon figures with evil eyes, great exaggerated fangs dripping blood, fantasy women with bared breasts, long-necked dragons, monsters with claw gauntlets, bulging-eyed demons and representations of famous Italians. Preceding each are brightly costumed men and women from the *contrada*.

The music is blasting, a sandstorm of noise that seems it could scour the stones and tiles of the buildings lining the narrow street.

These ghastly characters breathe smoke while their bodies, arms, legs and heads sway and writhe to some orchestrated automation as the hidden vehicle propelling them inches through the cobbled street and piazza. Thousands of people line this passageway of paganism, squeezed against the buildings as the floats pass by within inches, limbs, daggers and bloody swords plunging and soaring around them, threatening to impale them to some shop façade.

Their first march completed, the floats wheel and return along the same route. This is the signal to break out the confetti and goo fired from toy pistols. Within minutes, everyone is coated with these. And all the while, the music ricochets from building to building, from one end of the street to the other.

It was one of the most remarkable sights I have ever seen, unnerving, terrifying, mind-blowing, sense-numbing and exciting. The four fantasy floats of Foiano will long stay in my mind.

While Italy is the heart of the Roman Catholic world, it struggles at times to escape the pagan grip of the Etruscans and other peoples long since vanished. The church bells at the exact moment of the total eclipse of the moon on my first full night at San Clemente was my earliest experience of this. The Carnivale di Foiano reinforced this mystic link to a past where different gods and demons were worshipped or feared. Sometimes it seems the Church has even made some mysterious pact with this pagan past. The Explosion of the Cart was to be a revealing example.

Il Scoppio del Carro takes place in front of the Duomo of Florence each Easter Sunday morning. It is an amazing mixture of pomp and circumstance, church ritual, *contrade* competition, historical costuming, the First Crusade, and pagan fertility rites. I was to have a front-row seat to the spectacle. The cart is known as the *brindellone*, the Cart of St John, after St John the Baptist who is the patron saint of Florence. In the Middle Ages it was a rather small vehicle pulled by oxen the short distance from Piazza della Signoria to the space between the Duomo and the Baptistery. It carried a candle and made its short pilgrimage each June 24, the feast day of St John.

In time, it became a much more elaborate construction, a ten-metre high, four-metre wide, four-tiered tower. In it were niches for children to ride, and high on its peak stood a pelt-clad man representing St John. He was drawn from the ranks of the city's needy and paid ten lire for his troubles. He would eat, drink and throw money or tidbits to the crowd lining the route.

This annual ritual also has another Christian connection, dating back nine centuries to the First Crusade (1056–1100). One of the Florentine Crusaders, Pazzio de Pazzi, won eternal glory on a July day in 1099 when he apparently became the first Crusader to fight his way into the besieged city of Jerusalem. For this feat, he was awarded two pieces of silica from the Holy Sepulchre, which he brought back from his crusade to Florence. The silica was used as a flint to touch off a dove-shaped rocket erected near the altar of the great cathedral; it would 'fly' along a suspended wire to the stationed cart outside the Duomo's giant doors to ignite pre-positioned fireworks.

A successful ignition presaged a good harvest year as smoke and flame billowed around the forecourt of the cathedral. This introduced a pagan element to the event. The Church, insisting that the event is instead a symbol of the Resurrection, has clearly embraced the ceremony, with much pomp and circumstance and many prayer sessions leading up to the main event, the moment when the smoke-trailing dove crashes into the cart after its brief flight through the cathedral. In more modern times the organisers learned to appease the gods, the peasants and the tourists by ensuring the cart's ignition using a match or a cigarette lighter. On the day I witnessed the Explosion of the Cart, electrical wiring covered with sand snaked across the cobblestones from a nearby van to the cart. The miracle of electric power seems now to be used to perform the collective miracles of the dove, the explosion and the good harvest.

My Scoppio del Carro Easter Sunday began with the cheering news, as I drove up the autostrada, that it was only 4°C. The normally busy highway was eerily deserted but for a few cars and tourist campervans. I realised the difference was due to the absence of the trucks that flow so heavily along this main Italian artery. By the time I reached Florence the temperature had risen to 11°C but it had started to rain and blow a nasty wind. As I parked in a side street, I witnessed my own private Explosion of the Cart. Turning at the sound of muffled shouts, I saw a car just 50 metres away with its bonnet up and flames and smoke pouring out from the engine. The frantic driver was beating at the fire with a floor mat from the car. Each beat just fanned the blaze with renewed energy.

Before I had time to react, a young man came sprinting across the busy thoroughfare, fire extinguisher in hand. Within seconds he had doused the fire. The driver was lucky it was a well-maintained extinguisher; you hear so many stories of neglected extinguishers sitting in a wall bracket for years only to fail when an emergency finally arrives.

Because I had arranged a Press pass in advance, I had access to the inner sanctum of the Duomo forecourt, which was roped to keep back the rapidly growing crowd of spectators. A good 90 minutes before the 11 am kick-off for the main event, the cart arrived in this open space dragged by four large oxen garlanded with flowers. Because of the showers sweeping through the area, it was covered with a gigantic sheet of plastic to keep the explosives — fireworks — dry and ensure everything went as planned. The fireworks were artfully placed to avoid damaging the cart.

A parade of medieval-clad marchers, banner-wavers and soldiers tramped into the arena with much determination and trumpet-blowing. The Church arrived and disappeared with some dignitaries into the Baptistery for a prayer session, to emerge and walk around the cart, anointing it.

The blessing achieved, the Church retired and the crowd hushed. Suddenly, the 'dove', trailing a plume of white smoke, emerged at speed from the cathedral and smashed into the cart, which resembles a mobile and ornate tiered wedding cake. It took only an instant and then modern technology took over, triggering the hundreds of fireworks that had been carefully arranged inside and around the sides of the cart.

Catherine wheels screamed, firecrackers popped, thunder-crackers roared, skyrockets soared, and great cascades of sparks poured down the side of the vehicle. Clouds of coloured smoke issued from its interior, filling the forecourt. The noise was deafening, drowning the shrieks of delight and fright from the thousands of onlookers. Television crews and photographers rushed hither and to around the exploding vehicle, searching for that best angle. Some got alarmingly close.

I was standing perhaps ten metres from this raging scene. The light effect from the detonations was heightened by the gloom from the overcast sky. Later I would think it was an appropriate scene in the city of Dante. He no doubt witnessed it himself many times. I have seen many large public fireworks displays, Independence Day over Boston Harbour and Canada Day over Quebec's Plains of Abraham. What made this so different was the intimacy of it here in this small cobbled arena as great sheets of sound thundered off the walls of these historic buildings.

There was one last grand finale as red- and green-smoking rockets soared high into the Florentine sky.

As the explosions stopped, there were a few moments of absolute stillness and silence, the smoke seeping slowly away into the surrounding streets and alleys. The witnesses, including myself, were left overwhelmed by the spectacle. Then, a cacophony of excited noise rose from the crowd as it turned from awe to elation.

I turned to a man standing next to me and said simply, 'Spettacolare!'

'Si,' he replied with a wide smile now on his face.

He asked where I was from. When I told him he added, 'This is something only we in Italy have, perhaps only special thing. In New Zealand, you have rugby. We have this.' He stretched out his arms to encompass the scene, the now silent cart still smoking gently.

If the Foiano festival is bizarrely surreal and the Explosion of the Cart steeped in pagan and Church ritual, the barrel race of Montepulciano is an historical curiosity.

The Bravio delle Botti takes place each year on the last Sunday of August. Two-man teams representing each of the town's eight *contrade* compete by rolling 80 kg wine barrels over a 1.65 kilometre course to the central Piazza Grande. The winners receive the prized *bravio*, a scarlet drape of cloth with an iconoclastic image of the patron saint of the town, San Giovanni Battista Decollato. Originally, it was a horse race and today's version still follows the course through winding streets to the victory dais on the cathedral steps. As in the other towns of Tuscany, the streets in the old parts can be strenuous enough to walk. The effort these two-man teams or *spingitori* must put in seems murderous.

The race is preceded by a parade of some 200 people in 14th century costume. It follows the course of the race, stopping every now and then for a demonstration of banner throwing by each *contrada*, all dressed in their own 'colours', brilliant greens, yellows, blues and reds.

But the focus is on the barrels and the central square becomes packed with thousands of locals and tourists, a narrow path left by the crowd for the *spingitori* to negotiate the barrels. A large television screen is set up on a palace wall so progress can be monitored. Schoolchildren bedecked with their *contrade* flags and face-paint in the 'home team' colours gather in groups to cheer their side on. Dignitaries from public and church offices look down on the scene from their privileged places at the town hall windows. Friends call out to each other through the crowd; some experienced racegoers have bought portable chairs and secured prime front row spots. Apart from a small grandstand for the parade participants, we lesser mortals must mill and squeeze and crane for position and view.

At the tolling of the bells that signals the start of the race near the Porta al Prato entrance into the old town, a roar erupts from the gathered crowd. The honour of the *contrada* is at stake here. As word mysteriously spreads up to the square about who is leading, who is closing, who is lagging, cheers and groans echo through the square.

Finally, as the leading team arrives in the square and rolls its barrel up a ramp onto the top steps of the cathedral, bedlam breaks out among members of the winning *contrada*. They duck under or jump over the flimsy crowd control ropes and rush up the steps to embrace, hand-slap and kiss their victorious *spingitori*, who are too emotionally pumped to feel the pain of their effort. A line of police 'guarding' the top step is ignored as more and more spectators and media crews flood onto the stage. For several minutes, it is a scene of complete chaos, with further barrel teams arriving to add to the 'extras' on the set.

Later, leaving the scene, we pass an ambulance discreetly parked in a side street beside the cathedral. The crew is administering aid to jostled spectators and injured *spingitore*. It reminds me again of the fire in the belly the *contrade* system can generate.

From my earliest days in Italy I gathered calendars of events from the tourist offices that it seems each town, however small, boasts. Even little Trequanda has its own Pro Bono tourist information office where books, brochures, accommodation and local produce can be found. One festival that I looked into was the annual Grilli festival in Florence. My Italian-English dictionary informed me it was a cricket festival.

This, to my New Zealand eye, was good news. The game of cricket is the national summer sport in my home country.

As I knew cricket was not a game that Italians had taken to — its slow pace and duration would be too much for their passionate attitude to life — I thought it quite likely the expatriate community of cricket-playing nations could be involved. Perhaps the foreign diplomats and business representatives of Rome and Milan organised a fun day out in Florence, a chance to carry the cricket flag, picnic in the park and see the sights?

I mentioned the idea of getting together a party of cricket-nation expatriates in our area to go to the event and cheer our respective home sides on. This seemed an excellent prospect and I promised to gather more details. I contacted the Florence tourist office, expecting to hear the names of Australia, England,

South Africa mentioned as annual participants. The concept seemed quite conceivable to me. Only a few months before, in a small suburban shoe store on the very northern outskirts of greater Los Angeles, I had been served by an Indian (from the Asian subcontinent, that is) salesman. He picked up on my accent and we got talking about cricket. He said there was a strong cricket league played each week among the expatriate community that spreads itself through that vast collection of city-states. So I felt confident in my assumption that a similar gathering of like-minded souls was entirely possible in Italy. Unfortunately I was ignoring the advice of my first chief reporter when I was a nervous cadet reporter. 'Never assume on a newspaper, laddie,' he would admonish me with a wagging finger when I did just that.

The friendly young woman on the telephone was very helpful. Yes, she could tell me about the festival. It is in a park quite close to the centre of the city and was held each year for people to go to buy and sell crickets.

'They are in little cages and people go to get them as gifts for their children. The best ones to buy are the all black ones. They are the males and they make more noise than the females. After three days you will want to throw them away,' she added cheerfully.

'Why is that?' I asked.

'Because the noise in the house will drive you mad.'

So my cricket festival was of the chirping variety, not the off-spin as I had assumed. Quite what the origins of such an occasion could have possibly been I cannot begin to imagine. Suffice to say that I had no picnic in the park on the day the Festivale of Grilli came to Florence.

CHAPTER THIRTEEN

The Terracotta Capital of the World

AS A WORLD capital it is, frankly, rather pathetic. It has no White House or Lincoln Memorial, no Big Ben or Buckingham Palace, no Eiffel Tower or Arc de Triomphe.

Tiny Petroio, its close-ranked houses tumbling down a small, steep hill deep in southern Tuscany, can boast only a population of 450 souls, not the teeming millions of Moscow or Mexico City.

It has no public bar; the one watering hole is a private establishment run by the local branch of the Communist Party where old men gather to play cards on 1950s formica-and-stainless-steel tables in the afternoon. Schoolchildren and the few working-age young who have not fled town for the bright lights of the cities play video games upstairs. As this is a private establishment, its customers are presumably meant to be fully paid up Party members. But in the true spirit of capitalism, they will happily separate a thirsty *stranieri* from his lire.

There is no motorway network into the town, just a solitary entrance that leads to the sole 'main' street — wide enough for only one vehicle and squeezed by ancient houses as it spirals up and down the steep little hill with tiny alleys and arched stairways leading off from its cobbled route. Petroio cannot even muster the political muscle to be the 'capital' of the three-village local administrative district of which it is part; my nearby Trequanda with its population of about 900 claims that distinction.

Yet in this all-but-forgotten village in an all-but-forgotten part of the Tuscan landscape for hundreds — even thousands — of years, skilled artisans have hand-worked the clay that they discovered on the surrounding hilly slopes into burnt-orange shapes at once beautiful and practical. Today, the pots, vases, statues and urns that the tiny town produces grace gardens, hallways and patios in the most glamorous homes of the world.

Remarkably, the skilled hands of the craftsman are still his principal tool, just as they were thousands of years before Christ when the mysterious Etruscans first found their way to this part of Italy and discovered the rich veins of clay deposits created from the settling of sediment when this central part of Italy was under the sea. The legacy of that Pliocene era millions of years ago lies beneath the landscape of Le Crete, with its lonely farmhouses and lonelier cypress firs, between Petroio and Siena, 40 kilometres to the north.

No one knows how old Petroio is. The first 'modern' reference to 'Castro Petroio' was recorded in 1180 in the oldest archives of the bigger administrative centres of the area. It was one of the property holdings of the Cacciaconti family that dominated this area of southern Tuscany for centuries. References to the terracotta factories of the village date back to 1500, though 'factories' is altogether too grandiose a description; they were small, family-run workshops set up perhaps in a corner of a room in the house. Here, the craftsmen turned out an impressive range of products for both practical and ornamental use — massive jars for storing olive oil and wine, or for washing clothes beneath a charcoal filter, pots for the kitchen, vases, pipes for plumbing, chimney pots, small religious votives to embellish wall niches, coats-of-arms, statues . . .

Today, within the ancient remains of the town wall, descendants of these long-vanished artisans continue the traditions of the centuries. In cramped, dim, narrow buildings that have stood for a thousand years or more, they reach for a slab of slate-grey clay, about eighteen centimetres square and twelve centimetres thick. With a twirl of their hands, it becomes transformed into a long French bread roll. This they slap against the inside wall of a white plaster mould that will determine the shape, style, design and size of the final product after a weeks-long process. Block by clay block, the walls of the mould are built up by hand, moulded and knuckled with deft skill.

This is the critical part of the production process. The clay must be just the right thickness — too thin and it will crack in the searing heat of the kiln; too thick and it will not 'cook' right through. Yet these craftsman have no tools or measures to help them. They rely on 'feel' and on experience to know when the clay is at just the right thickness. It is a skill that takes years to learn, just as it has taken centuries for this knowledge to be passed from generation to generation, father to son to grandson.

The story of a Petroio terracotta item begins in a quarry on a hillside overlooking the Valdichiana, the valley of the Chiana River, that leads south to Rome and north to Florence. It has long been a principal route linking the Eternal City with the towns and cities of northern Italy and, beyond the Alps, the rest

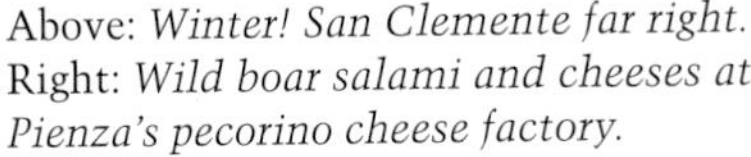

Above: *Winter! San Clemente far right.*
Right: *Wild boar salami and cheeses at Pienza's pecorino cheese factory.*

Autumn

Above left: *Casa Nova, a reminder of a centuries-old peasant farming way of life.* Above right: *Mineral mud at the pool of Bagno Vignoni.*

Below left: *Floats of Foiano.* Below right: *The Explosion of the Cart in front of Florence's duomo (cathedral).*

Above: *Petroio, the terracotta capital of the world.*

Below left: *Montepulciano's abbey of San Biagio glows in the setting sun.* Below right: *A curious order from a terracotta factory in Petroio.*

Above: *Making good use of the wild blackberry harvest.*

Below left: *The most beautiful bride . . .* Below right: *Sinalunga's big October market day.*

of Europe. Along its valley floor and through the hills above have travelled Etruscans, Romans, Carthaginians led by Hannibal, and French and Barbarian invaders. As recently as half a century ago, another invading army brought the arms of modern mechanised war to the valley only to be forced back to its native Germany by an even stronger invading force. The battle front passed through the woods, hills and lanes where today the locals pursue more peaceful endeavours and harvests than that of violent death — rich olive oil, lusty wines, fruits and vegetables and the clay to feed the waiting kilns of Petroio.

The open quarry scars the hillside I drive by each day as machines slice out their grey gold in vertical layers like some giant tiered wedding cake. The excavated clay is then left to weather for some nine months, or to 'decant' as the process is more correctly called. After this decanting period, the clay is ground, pugged and mixed with water to soften it for the waiting artisans just a few kilometres away in their ancient workshops of Petroio. By this stage, it is exhibiting the properties that make Le Crete clay so suitable for producing terracotta — plasticity, malleability, porosity and hardening.

The only tools the craftsman uses are his hands and a small square of wafer-thin flexible plastic — hands for rolling the clay slabs and then punching it into the mould, the plastic for smoothing and, with its sharp edge, trimming. The range of products and designs is extensive. Some are metre-high, metre-wide containers for lemon trees, others are delicate little pots more suited for herb plants. Some are tall and elegant, others squat and square. There are statues of lions, ornamental pine cones for gate posts, masks and the distinctive chimney pots of the Tuscan house. Outside one Petroio factory stands a line of Snow White and the seven dwarfs, curious leftovers from a bizarre order by an Austrian company.

A large urn or pot may take up to two hours to mould. The biggest have to be formed in several moulds which are then joined so the craftsman can work the separate clay shapes into a whole for the firing. The clay is then left in the mould for some hours — the time depends on the size — to let it lose some moisture and shrink. Over this period, it will reduce in size by nearly 10 per cent and it can then be pulled neatly from the mould.

After a final smoothing and trim, it is stored away for up to three weeks to dry out completely. It is now ready for the kiln. Great stacks of prepared, dried products are piled into the kiln's chamber and, once the doors are sealed, the kiln is fired to 1000°C for 24 hours. But it will be days — up to five — before the kiln chamber cools and can be opened for the fired products to be removed.

These are now ready for the last process, 'tinning'. They are stored and soaked continuously with running water for a day or more to wash out any remaining impurities in the clay. Then, finally, the sienna-orange terracotta vases or pots or statues are completed.

The art of terracotta, like so many other art forms, began to flourish in earnest in the Renaissance, which was born in the Tuscan capital of Florence some 100 kilometres to the north of Petroio. It is no coincidence that the early records of terracotta-making in Petroio date back to that era. The artists of the time of that cultural rebirth began to experiment with designs based on ancient themes as well as bold new decorations and styles. The aim was to combine the grand driving imperatives of the Renaissance — culture, beauty, nature, practicality and civilised living. Beautiful parks and gardens were laid out, great buildings like the Duomo in Florence were designed and built, whole towns like Pienza were constructed. In this liberal environment, the ancient traditions of terracotta were also transformed.

Today, that 'new-look' tradition of terracotta remains and the products of Petroio incorporate a wide range of artistic and historic influences as well as utility — leaves and masks of satyrs from the villa gardens of ancient Rome, urns with influences from ancient Greece, crests and coats-of-arms from the great families of the Renaissance who became patrons of the artists (the crest of the all-powerful Medici family is a common feature), garlands of wheat, grapes and olives to reflect the larder that is the Tuscan countryside, statues of beautiful maidens and proud lions . . .

The old artists had their pride, too, in their craftsmanship. Products were inscribed with a nail or some other tool before the firing to assure buyers of its quality and its creator. Today that same pride remains with each craftsman responsible for taking a particular product through the entire pre-firing production process — moulding, smoothing, finishing and trimming.

It is also matched by the pride of the factories that employ them and the town where they live. In the last years of the millennium, the terracotta businesses have formed a consortium to promote, protect and preserve the image, quality and genuineness of their collective products. Instead of a nail, a stamp bearing Petroio's name is now stamped into the soft clay. A terracotta museum is being developed in the town and in 1998 an inaugural annual terracotta festival was held.

Petroio's oldest terracotta factory has been making its products for at least 250 years under the ownership of one family, the Benocci family.

'We know it is at least that old from dates inscribed on oil jars,' says Raffaella Benocci, wife of the young Maurizio Benocci who is the latest generation to help run the business. His father and brother also work for the firm. She says a pot dated 1660 and discovered in the city of Arezzo across the Valdichiana valley also bears the Benocci name, 'but we don't know if it was from our family'.

As if to proclaim its heritage as the town's oldest terracotta factory, it also features the town's tallest structure — a distinctive brick kiln chimney that soars some three stories above the cramped, gloomy floorspace of the factory. This overhangs a deep gully on one edge of the town, looking across to a densely wooded hillside.

The premises are about 200 metres inside the long-gone town gate where a cross of the Knights Templar still stands guard on the town wall. Inside, the small band of craftsmen skirt around white plaster moulds littering the wooden floor ('We have the moulds made in Florence'), stacks of drying products waiting to be fired and pallets of clay slabs as they work at tables or upended boxes creating their latest product. In one corner, a modern oil-fired kiln has somehow been squeezed in.

In conservative, Catholic Italy, traditions resist change; the 'old way of doing it' is still seen to be the best. In rural Tuscany, this holds particularly true. So the kiln represents a major leap of faith into the new technology for the Benocci family.

'Until 25 years ago, we still used wood to fire the kiln but the cooking was not so uniform,' says Raffaella.

It was only in 1995 that this modern kiln was installed.

'With the old kiln, each time [of the firing] it would be sealed up with bricks which would then be broken down to get the pots out.'

Today, just five factories operate inside the old town walls. But over the years, new ones have sprung up in the 'new town' that has spread outside as population growth has continued. They have also spread to nearby towns and villages like Trequanda and Pienza.

Even the Benocci works have expanded, with two large

plants in the nearest major town, Sinalunga. Together, they provide much-needed work for eighteen people who produce an astonishing volume of products for such a labour-intensive industry. The business has expanded in other ways, too. After the last war it began looking for new markets throughout Europe and by 1960 it had established a now-strong base in the United States. Newer markets have since been found in more distant countries such as Australia and Japan.

In this way, Petroio has created links with the other great capitals of the world. Its products grace handsome mansions, exclusive apartments and sculptured gardens in London, Paris and Madrid as well as the narrow windowsills and alleyways of its own village. Beyond that, they can be found in the homes of the super-rich of Los Angeles, New York, Sydney and Miami . . . not bad for a tiny little Tuscan town of less than 500 residents.

CHAPTER FOURTEEN

The War Comes to San Clemente

'FIVE GERMAN SOLDIERS were killed here by the Americans. They were buried in that field there but pigs came and dug them up. After the war their bodies were taken away.'

For a few brief days in the autumn of 1944 the insanity of World War II came to San Clemente and to Trequanda. It was a violent and bloody visit.

The Italians had already surrendered when the Germans came down the lane to San Clemente. Even then, the war was effectively over as Allied soldiers pushed them relentlessly northward up the Italian boot. Monte Cassino had been destroyed, Rome had been liberated and slowly the Allied forces — a pre-United Nations mix of Americans, British, Anzacs, South Africans and other nations — were pushing north from the Eternal City.

Finally, the front came to Tuscany and San Clemente. Elario was able to recount its passage in vivid detail. I had already brought him back to the home of his boyhood; now I sat in the dining room of his retirement apartment, looking over the valley to his vineyard and olive grove as he brought those brief but tumultuous days back to life.

As we talked, we drank the wine that Elario had made from his vines. Eva brought us an unending stream of dried grapes and figs. The figs had been dried in an underground hole dug into a bank on Elario's small patch of land. 'You put figs on tray and every day light fire underneath. Every day, and after week figs are nice and dry,' he told us. There was also a delicious 'cake' of figs, aniseed and almonds that he had made.

Elario has done well for himself. Eva is a charming, house-proud and hospitable hostess with a ready laugh. She is too young to have known the war. I wondered what horror her parents and grandparents endured through those years. Poland was a killing ground — there was the burning of Warsaw, the Warsaw uprising, Nazi invasion and Russian counterattack. Many of the Holocaust camps worked furiously at their grisly business within its borders.

But today I want to hear what happened when the war came to San Clemente.

The war had already touched Elario and his family. His brother had been conscripted into the Italian Army. The Government took most of the produce the farm produced to feed its forces — 'We were left with only a small, small bit.' But until the late summer and early autumn of 1944, the fighting stayed away from the peaceful hills of San Clemente.

The first they knew of it was the sound of bombing raids at the strategic town of Arezzo, across the Valdichiana, the rumble of distant artillery fire and, at night, the bright light of parachute flares over the valley floor below — 'very beautiful,' remembered Elario. 'But the bombing make a scare in the night.' The family prepared for the war to come to their world. They made hiding places for their food — prosciutto and cheeses were concealed beneath the tiles at the top of the villa's stairway. Wines and oil were sealed up behind bricks in what is now the kitchen window. Other goodies were secreted in a haystack. The chickens and pigs were taken deep into the woods. 'The German soldiers pinch everything. If the German soldier was hungry, he would take everything.' And the family made preparations to guard itself as well as its treasures. Elario and his brother dug a shelter into the bank below the summer garden, a horseshoe with two entrances just metres from the back of the house and facing away from the approaching fighting. 'Dig like miner. Was hard ground.' The pair and their two sisters used this shelter. The rest of the family would spend nights in a centuries-old escape chamber built by friars at Miciano, the big house further down the lane. It was excavated 'when religions were killing each other' but today little remains of it, just a hole in the ground. There, while the bombs dropped over Arezzo and the artillery roared just metres from the walls of San Clemente, Elario's family and the two families who lived at Miciano would huddle in the refuge, perhaps three metres by three metres square.

Providing a refuge from the violence and death was becoming a normal part of life. For a time the family sheltered two Italian generals and a colonel, along with a dog they had actually taken to the savagery of the Russian front with its bitter cold and bitter fighting. Evidently, they became sick of the whole business of war and decided to take cover at San Clemente. But the 'Fascisti' were looking for them to press them back into the fighting with the Germans. 'They didn't want to go. We were worried that somebody might spy the dog so my brother killed it.'

Eventually they departed, leaving four pistols and ammunition that the family hid in the woods. Later they returned to collect two of the guns.

These were dangerous and cruel times. While German troops were stationed at San Clemente for only four days, they were an increasing presence in the area as the war came closer. 'There, in *i monti, partigiani* killed a German soldier,' said Elario, pointing to My Lady of the Mountains from the window. 'The Germans burnt down a house where the *partigiani* stayed, so they captured the soldier and shot him. He said, "Please don't kill me. I married, have children." But they killed him.'

Escaping prisoners of war also came to San Clemente. Elario remembers three English soldiers — 'Lieutenant Stewart [or Stuart], George and Frank' — who had been released with other prisoners from their prison camp after the Italian surrender. 'They open gates and say, "You go."' Somehow, they made their way to San Clemente. They stayed at Miciano but would eat with Elario's family. He remembers dance evenings at Miciano: 'Lieutenant Stewart would play the harmonica.'

He also recalls the officer had a secret compartment in his belt where he had pound notes hidden. They would change it into Italian lire at a bank in Sinalunga.

After a month or so, they heard that the Fascists were looking for them so went on their way. But the head of the Miciano family that sheltered them was arrested by the Fascists and spent four months in prison in Bologna.

In recent years, Elario has thought often about trying to find the three soldiers — 'all from London, I think' — through newspapers. Perhaps this book may help?

Even Elario's brother, the only one conscripted into the army, had to hide. After the 8 September surrender of the Italians he left the army but was picked up by German troops who wanted to press him back into service. 'But he escape again and come to San Clemente. He hide in a haystack but come into house at night. For a month or more.'

And finally the Germans came to *i monti*. One autumn

morning, the family heard the clatter of hooves, neighing of horses, clank of metal and voices of a foreign language coming down the lane from the Petroio-Trequanda road that cuts across *i monti*. It was a horse-drawn artillery unit manned by some 100 soldiers. 'Lots and lots of horses.'

They had come north as the Allied advance emerged from Rome and began the drive for Florence. By the time the artillery unit arrived, the Allies had already captured Montepulciano and were nearing Pienza. This, said Elario, was the German gunners' target.

The Germans swiftly erected camouflage tents along where the southern fence now separates San Clemente from the neighbouring field. Under these they set up their guns, aimed south towards that beautiful town — our town.

More artillery was placed at the Abbadia Sicile, high on a ridgeline to the south; I can see its outline as I write now by the front door in the winter sun. Another unit was stationed in the olive grove of my neighbour, Airdrie; I can also see her house from San Clemente. Fittingly, perhaps, the sound of violent death echoes around me as the warm day has brought hunters to my woods in big numbers. Their rifle shots are as nothing compared to the sound the guns must have made as they roared from beneath their netting just metres from San Clemente's walls. They were hunting bigger, more dangerous game — Allied soldiers, tanks, supply lines and guns.

The Germans led their horses and the family's cattle into the woods. By now the Allied airforce controlled the sky over southern Tuscany and a large concentration of animals spotted by a searching pilot would bring fighters and bombers to these normally peaceful fields. Because the artillery was far behind the front line and the actual fighting (20 or so kilometres behind!), there was no immediate danger except from the air. But the hidden animals and camouflage netting proved effective. So the family stayed in the house even though the soldiers commandeered all the bedrooms. 'We sleep in kitchen,' said Elario. In a house where every room had a purpose in those days of the *mezzadria*, it was the only available space.

Life at the farm, then, continued in its normal pattern. This was harvest season. The grapes had to be picked, the grain gathered, the orchards cleared, the fields ploughed. But this was not a normal time and the roar of the artillery sent shock waves through the fields and woods.

'Boom! Wheeee! Boom! Wheeee!' recalled Elario.

Despite the tension, the fear, the pungent smell of cordite, the roar of death that must have filled the air of San Clemente, the Germans did not treat the family badly. 'They not nasty to us. Quite nice people.' They even showed some sympathy for their hosts' plight in the everyday battle for survival. The family had hidden more foodstuffs — prosciutto, cheeses — in the big haystack where Elario's brother had been concealed for a month. 'One day, the Germans went to get hay for the horses from it. One soldier said to us we should move the prosciutto if we didn't want the horses to eat them!'

And then, after four days, the Germans left. They gathered their kit, took down the netting, collected their hidden horses, limbered their guns and went back up the lane. Who knows where? Did they survive the war? Are they alive today?

Now the real danger began for the family as the front proper came to Petroio, San Giovanni d'Asso, Montisi, Trequanda, the towns I know so well. These were the days and nights when the people huddled fearfully in caves or shelters like the one Elario and his brother dug. The English and Commonwealth troops were driving up the Valdichiana. Moroccan forces were advancing through the Val d'Asso, on the other side of *i monti*. It fell to the GIs to come through Petroio, along the top road and on into Trequanda.

Always ahead of them were the retreating German soldiers, fighting fiercely to slow the advance, hoping, probably, for some miracle.

Isolated pockets of retreating Germans came through the woods and across the fields. One day, one of Elario's brothers spotted a group of three above San Clemente. 'He say come on, take sickle. We cut their neck. So I pick up sickle like him and we go out.'

It was, by any reckoning, a foolhardy venture — two people armed with grain-cutting sickles setting out on their own little war against three armed, battle-experienced and desperate soldiers fighting for their lives every inch of their retreat.

Fortunately Elario's father spied the two would-be warriors from an upstairs window. 'He say where you going. When we tell him he say are we crazy, get back here at once!'

The front passed along the road above San Clemente. At the bend that today marks the entrance to Airdrie's house stands her olive grove. Americans shot and killed the three Germans there.

The arrival of the Allies at San Clemente itself was rather an anticlimax.

'One or two Americans just walk down the road to house. No jeep, no tank. If Germans still in woods, they be killed straight away. But they not frightened,' he said, still obviously amazed at the victors' casual attitude.

After the obligatory hand-out of cigarettes and chocolates, the Americans moved on towards Trequanda. 'They ask, "Any Germans here?" Then they go, don't stop.'

The departing Germans left explosive memories for the local people to remember their passing. At Montisi they destroyed a slender 600-year-old tower, similar to the one in Siena's Il Campo, that was built in the ancient Grancia, a fortified farm with moats, drawbridge, oil presses, cellars and a cloister. The commanding view from the top of the tower was, apparently, too strategic to be left for enemy use. They tried, too, to blow up the round tower of the castle at Trequanda. It has since been restored, unlike the one at Montisi. They also planted a large mine at the bottom of the steep little hill that takes you up into the old town. Today, there is no evidence of any destruction it might have created. Nor is there anywhere else among the hills and forests of *i monti*.

At San Clemente, the shelter that Elario built 'like miner' has long since collapsed, the food hiding place at the top of the stairs is permanently tiled, the kitchen window is unbricked and floods the room with morning sun. The Germans who now come to Trequanda bring marks, not guns. They sit in the summer sun of Piazza Garibaldi and gaze unknowingly at the tower that was blown up by their retreating countrymen. And today's Americans bring neither cigarettes nor candy; their offering is much more prized — the sweet taste of the dollar.

Old soldiers like to return to their battlefields to remember and to mourn. Have any of those who passed by here in those violent days of 1944 returned? Probably not. Trequanda, *i monti*, San Clemente — these were but blinks in the war's eye. The land continues to go calmly about its business as it has over the centuries despite the death, destruction and violence so often brought to it. The olives still produce their oil, the vines their grapes, the fields their grain. With the wisdom of nature, the land can contemptuously ignore these petty affairs of men.

But for Elario, and the other people who lived here through those times, the memory is still vivid; they were desperate days. The war ended but in its wake there was little celebration. 'Church bell ring for hours and hours. Everybody so upset. So many people killed.'

CHAPTER FIFTEEN

'The People You Meet . . .'

THE BEAUTY OF any country is measured as much by its people as its landscape. My Italian world is peopled with two distinct populations, *i stranieri* and locals. I am one of the *stranieri*, the foreigners.

Like the Chianti hills north of Siena, the landscape of southern Tuscany has drawn people from many countries. Some, vacationing holidaymakers, return year after year for their few weeks of leave. Others come to stay, perhaps after a vacation visit. They may set up home in one of the abandoned farmhouses of the long-gone *mezzadria*. Or they may take an apartment in the hamlets and towns that lie scattered around me.

They come from Germany, England, France, America, Australia, Finland. Some have been here for twenty years or more. Others like myself are new kids on the Tuscan block. They come — and stay — for countless reasons. Perhaps they have fled a failed relationship. Perhaps they are escaping a city commuter's life. They may be seeking the peace of a rural lifestyle or be travellers who have found a place to settle for a while. Many have an artistic bent — painting, sculpting, writing, music, woodworking. They all, however, share a love of the land. From their ranks I will make friends and develop a social life.

A large number of the expatriates are independently wealthy. But those who need an income scratch a living through a variety of means — handyman jobs, renting out rooms, hosting Italian cooking and culture classes for Japanese or Americans, teaching music, selling artwork, helping at the grape and olive harvests . . . much of it is 'black' or undeclared cash income. It can be a precarious financial lifestyle but the riches in the landscape that surrounds us all are reward enough for most.

One of my earliest such contacts was with a German husband and wife, Reiner and Hannalore Traub, who were to become good friends. Both tall and lean, they live in rather splendid isolation in a refurbished *mezzadria* house on the other side of Trequanda from San Clemente. Standing by one of the old entrance gates to the village, I can see their house high atop a hill, perhaps a kilometre away, surrounded by steeply falling farmland. Beyond, the towers of Siena are visible on a clear day.

Like many other of the Tuscan expatriates they came initially for a brief visit, in their case a year, but stayed and stayed . . . and stayed. When I first met them, they had been in their hilltop eyrie for seven years. They eke a living in a variety of ways. Both make jewellery, which they sell in Germany. In the season they also rent out two renovated apartments that are part of their villa complex.

Like life at San Clemente, theirs is an isolated existence so they welcome opportunities to go out for an evening and that is how I come to play pool with them in local villages. I am able to introduce them to the ether of the Internet so they can keep up with the local holiday apartment competition. In this way I can repay them for their kindness when they try to help repair things that break down around the house. In any rural community, people will come to your aid; in a foreign land this assistance is doubly welcome.

One summer twilight I forgot to turn off the jeep's lights on coming home from town. Sure enough, the battery was as flat as a supermodel's chest the next morning. I tried to jumpstart it by rolling backwards out of our sharp little drive. Not a peep. We then repeated the procedure down the lane where it dips below San Clemente. Still nothing. Parking the car as near to the fence as possible to allow any other vehicles to get by on the one-vehicle lane, I prepared to trudge back to the house to summon help, perhaps Reiner with jump cables or a lift to town.

All the while a bulldozer had been working in the distant field. The driver obviously could see that something was amiss and came clanking across. I explained about the battery. He promptly manoeuvred the big machine so close to the fence and car that we were able to pass jump leads through the wires and revive the jeep. Such is the way of things in the country.

I was able to perform some modest little Samaritan services myself — putting together a kitset gas heater for a neighbour; ferrying people to and from the garage for their cars to be repaired. One day at the top of the lane I came across a young couple holidaying from Dresden in the former East Germany. They were standing helplessly in the top field next to their car. It had been raining quite heavily for a day or two and the inevitable happened when they decided to drive their car out into the field to admire the always spectacular view.

The car was well and truly stuck. My visiting cousin and I went down to the villa and returned with some stout rope. But even with the four-wheel-drive engaged we could not budge it;

we simply could not get enough traction on the slick grass and mud.

So we drove a kilometre towards town and pulled into the main farm complex where the Chianina beef are raised, fed and housed. I was able to explain the situation and the farmer duly arrived with his tractor, which solved the problem quickly. He was not impressed; hunters on foot are tolerated but to drive a car onto the farmland was overstepping the mark, even for these two obvious city dwellers. He also glowered at me, presuming I suppose that they were my guests.

Quite what possessed them to try their luck I have no idea. Even city folk must surely realise that water, grass and soil make an eel-like trinity. But they were grateful and brought a thank-you bottle of grappa to the house a couple of days later.

From San Clemente, I can look up to *i monti* and see the house of my neighbour, Airdrie. At night, the light from her kitchen window is a warming beacon, a signal that I am not alone here in my isolated environment. She is Irish and like her fellow compatriots is warm-hearted, with an ever-ready smile, and sparkling eyes. But these mask a deep sadness; shortly before my arrival her husband Mario, a wealthy and influential Italian banker, died suddenly. It seemed a double tragedy because Airdrie is one of those people who reaches out to give much love to those she knows.

She is a great entertainer and supports young people with artistic talent. It is at her dinner parties and musical evenings that I meet many *stranieri* and locals from the towns nearby. During my first summer Airdrie sponsored a school for promising young musicians at her home, paying for the airfares for those who could not afford it, providing their board and arranging for a leading Italian music teacher to give them tuition. The students, in their early 20s, were an enthusiastic and friendly crowd; there was even a young Kiwi flautist, who just before coming here broke his hand and was unable to play his instrument during his stay. But he soaked up the atmosphere and the opportunity to learn his craft alongside his musical peers — singers, pianists, cellists.

The 'price' of their stay was two concerts in the church of San Pietro and Sant'Andreo in Trequanda. We joined the audience that packed the church for one of these free evenings. They were indeed a talented group and one day will fill the concert halls and opera theatres of the world; a measure of the talent can be gauged by the fact that San Clemente's owner, Carlo, had auditioned one for a part in one of his operas.

Later, Airdrie was to provide a home for a promising young English artist, Elizabeth Cochrane, who was able to have an exhibition of her work in the ancient castle at San Giovanni d'Asso during the annual truffle festival.

Airdrie was not only a collector of musical talent. She also collected waifs and strays. Her kitchen/dining room — a glorious clutter of hanging cookware, herbs, posters, comfortable old sofas and a majestic wooden dining table — was a home for stray cats and dogs she somehow rescued from a less hospitable home. She even collected human strays like Sam, the Englishwoman who fled from an unpromising relationship into a slavish Italian domestic one, caring for an elderly, waspish woman. Sam with her ready laugh and I become friends and enjoyed many outings before the absence of her daughter back in England became too compelling and she returned to her homeland.

They were an eclectic crowd, the people I met at Airdrie's soirées. I remember vividly the big-bodied, big-voiced Englishman and his Swedish wife, equally big in stature — not fat, just big with the kind of voice and presence that occupies a room rather than a chair. They had a ghastly little black dog that was astoundingly oversexed; I cannot remember the breed but it was like a miniature bulldog — all nose and wheeze. They delighted in bringing this horrid little creature into the house where it spent an hour or so desperately trying to mount Airdrie's Alsatian bitch. It was a battle of the sexes the damned thing was doomed to lose; its head barely reaching the Alsatian's knee. At first it was great sport to watch but as the minutes rolled on the poor thing's desperation became embarrassing and loathsome. Its owners thought this was great sport while the rest of the gathered company squirmed with increasing discomfort. At one stage they put a lead on it and the sex-crazed animal nearly choked as it strained against its leash and collar to reach its *objet d'amour*, great gasping breaths erupting from it as it paused for air in its exertions.

If Airdrie's was at once a social pool and a melting pot, a Times Square of rural Tuscany — Guiseppe the writer trying, like me, to find a publisher or agent, Laura the English author, who had an agent and a lover, the Italian builder who stayed on — it was also a place to meet some of the local Italians socially. Some I would be introduced to for the first time, but others I knew from Trequanda. These were the folk I would have to deal with in my daily routine.

There was the dark-haired, moustached, flashing-eyed Ivano at the co-op grocery store. He likes to flirt with the ladies but was at first distant with this newcomer. There were young Fabio and Sylvia from the Piazza Garibaldi's Emporium, where I would buy my copy of the *International Herald Tribune*. I must have passed some test the night I met them at Airdrie's; before then I was greeted with a formal 'buon giorno' but the next morning and thenceforth it was to be the friendly and accepting, 'Ciao, Allan'. There was also Luca, the young, curly-haired vet, who would wave to me as I went about my business.

Like the French, the Italians have a formal and an informal way of addressing and greeting people. It is important to let them take the lead in this decision-making process; you are after all a guest in their home country. The engaged couple at my local *macelleria*, the butcher shop, treated me quite differently. Enrico, the owner, began saying 'ciao' after about six months. But his fiancée, Rosanna, herself a qualified butcher, would still use 'arrivederla' even after a year. This is the formal version of the widespread 'arrivederci' that most people use, between acquaintances as well as friends. Enrico and Rosanna must be the longest engaged couple in history — fifteen years, I was told, and still living with their respective parents. Even within the strictures of Catholic Italy, that is a *long* wait.

Enrico is a tall, thin — almost gaunt — hook-nosed man and it was always a joy to watch his skill as he deboned a leg of prosciutto or lamb. The quality of their meat was excellent, although the beef was not aged well, perhaps an Italian trait. To be sure, the sight of a skinned whole rabbit with head and eyes still intact, or a chicken with head and feet still attached, was initially alarming to my more Western eyes. But this was just a cultural, not a hygienic, difference. It was also odd to find wine, jam, preserves, cheese and pasta for sale in a butcher shop, but again this was commonplace. Enrico could, in fact, teach lessons about cleanliness and presentation to many butchers in my native New Zealand.

My main problem in buying my meat was knowing what it all was. Not only were the cuts of meat different but they had mystifying Italian names. Over time, Enrico and I would begin swapping English and Italian names — mince for *macinato, cosci di pollo* for chicken legs, and so on. In this and other ways, I began slowly to learn about my new country, its language and its people.

Next door to Enrico is the 'Bar Paradiso', the place to be seen on weekend nights by the town's small teen population. It is a combination *gelateria*, bar and café. The owner is Giorgio, a tall, well-exercised, shaven-headed man of about 30 years. The Bar Paradiso's walls are lined with black-and-white posters of American scenes and the music of American groups rings through its two rooms. Giorgio hopes to establish a *gelateria* in the States and at the end of my first year was returning there with hopes of achieving just that in Las Vegas's Caesar's Palace, through a contact he made during a winter sojourn in San Francisco and Arizona.

During the summer months, when tourist cars vied with the residents for parking space, a comical little running battle developed between the local sheriff and myself. The constable or Polizia Municipale is Signor Maurilio Graziani. He is one of the seventeen-strong workforce of the Comune de Trequanda, or local town council, and has an office fronting onto the village's central Piazza Garibaldi. He is rather like a bulldog — thick and stout in a way that suggests he is doomed to the stooped bandy-leggedness that seems to be a genetic inheritance in Mediterranean climes. He always looks very trim in his immaculately pressed uniform. Our sheriff is not to be confused with the omnipresent, omnipotent national police, the Carabinieri, who also have a station in the village. These are serious cops, police with attitude, while Signor Graziani's role is a more placid one — issuing permits for public entertainment, dog licensing, maintaining an 'official' presence at religious festivals, approving closing hours for bars and restaurants . . . On occasions he will be drafted in to be an extra on-site 'hand' at big events in some other town, the annual market day in downtown Sinalunga, for example, or the annual white truffle festival in San Giovanni d'Asso. These affairs always have an impressive turn-out of orange-coated, radio-equipped, direction givers, town police and Carabinieri. They are also very peaceful, just a bunch of happy Italians enjoying an outing. It seems ludicrous that they need to bring in outside 'help'. In peaceful little Trequanda, where the Bar La Siesta's video games are the liveliest entertainment, his task is not an onerous one. This gives him ample time to focus on what appears to be the primary joy of his role, policing the town's parking spots. It is in this 'parking monitor' role that he and I were to close battle.

Halfway up the hill to the main *piazza*, there is a large parking area (taken over when the travelling circus comes to town and spreads its Big Top across it). But it is a stiff walk up past the castle walls and most people prefer to try their luck at the small parking place behind the town hall building. Here one is able to park for an hour, using the ubiquitous window disc system that operates here. When I first arrived, there was space for perhaps ten or twelve cars. Incomprehensibly, these limited spaces were reduced during my first year. One space disappeared under the white lines of a pedestrian crossing to the public toilet at the rear of the town hall. Another two vanished with some town planner's grand scheme to build a large standing area by the public water tap where people come to fill their bottles.

The angled parking spaces that remained were prime real estate, particularly in the busy summer months. Trequanda has its own tiny one-way system. You drive up the hill past the castle on the left, turn into the road with these parking spaces and then into the little alley between the town hall and church which brings you into the *piazza*. To leave, you drive through the old entrance way between the bank and the castle church, into the same road you ascended to come into town. So every vehicle passes these parking spaces. When they are full, some people park opposite them, hard against the little fence that encloses the small park. This still leaves room for incoming traffic to get through into the square. Of course this is forbidden territory for our sheriff, who polices this and the square with earnest vigilance, full of capped and sunglassed importance in the finest tradition of a Los Angeles cop (mercifully, he has not yet taken to gum-chewing). He will emerge from his office, eyeball the square for any errant parkers there and then stride around to check out vehicular miscreants in this 'back street lot'. This is important work! And official business! The 'streets of Laredo' must be kept clean!

He would adopt a strategic position at the exit from the *piazza* from which he could see traffic coming into town and note if it then emerged into the *piazza*. If not, it was a mere stroll of five metres to find out if the missing vehicle had parked legally (against the town hall building) or illegally (against the park fence).

This was an impressive advance in the apparently ceaseless fight against street (-parking) crime in Trequanda. Here was a man with a role, a mission and a plan. And I was to become his victim and his project to protect the town.

As the early summer sun blazed down one day, I took my chances and parked in this 'no go' zone, daunted by the prospect of the uphill climb from the car park below. I had not reckoned on Sig. Graziani's enthusiastic vigilance. I left the car for maybe ten minutes beside the park fence to do my shopping. When I returned I noticed him at the far end of the street and, sure enough, as I drove out of the *piazza* to leave, he was waiting in ambush. He held up his hand in the universal stop signal and told me I must not park there. 'Mi dispiace, I'm sorry,' I told him. 'Va bene, okay'; never again, I promised. And with that modest reproach I was let free.

On another occasion I left the car longer than the officially-ordained five minutes in the Piazza Garibaldi itself. This too earned a finger-waving protest with an admonition that I must be more prompt in the future.

I became a miscreant yet again when I failed to pull the car far enough into a parking space to satisfy the meticulous Sig. Graziani. As I returned laden with grocery bags he strode towards me, shrugging his shoulders, eyes skyward for solace and hands alternately outstretched or making a 'too far out' gesture. 'What am I going to do with you?' He had decided to adopt me as his special project, to bring all his official bearing on this crime-wave of a foreigner until I toed the line.

And so our cat-and-mouse contest continued. But in its own way it became a friendly game. After a time I would earn a smile and the prized 'ciao' greeting as we passed each other in his territory, the *piazza*. One day, leaving the town, he stopped me in the car. 'What have I done now?' I thought. But he just wanted to let me know that there was a letter for me in the town post office (my mail address is normally a post office box in Sinalunga). It was a friendly gesture that I appreciated but it was also a salutary lesson that, like any small town anywhere, everybody knows who you are and more so if you are a foreigner.

Directly opposite the constable's office is the retail outlet for a local artist, one of the most outrageous poseurs I have ever seen. In my first months, I would observe him ride into town from his house just outside the town, clad in riding habit and knee-length boots and self-importantly erect on his white horse. He would stop outside his display shop and wait for his wife to come running out with a cup of coffee, which he would drink with studied nonchalance astride the animal. Perhaps he had a Rhett Butler complex.

Later, I was to remark on this phenomenon of pomposity and arrogance to friends. 'When did you last see it?' they asked. 'About a year ago,' I replied. 'Ah, that's about when his wife left him.' I was not at all surprised.

I also commented on the wide range of art in different styles he produced. There was always an impressive array on show.

'That's because he copies it from magazines and photos.'

I was to become familiar with the faces of Trequanda: the 'whistler', the cabinet maker whose whistled arias and concertos were so loud they rang throughout the *piazza*, the fast-striding pharmacist with his flowing mane of wavy white hair trying to keep pace behind him, the cheerful, ever-grinning visage of the man behind the counter at the post office. Beyond, in Sinalunga, I was to become acquainted with other faces — the fussing and smiling old ladies who ran the magazine shop, the coquettish eyes of the clerks at the Post Office, the beaming smile of our Internet provider, Ivan. And, above all, the warmth of the welcome from the team at the fruit and vegetable stall, Claudio, Fiorella and Doni — their eyes and smiles seemed to light up with a special delight when I arrived. Claudio had a deliciously wicked sense of humour. One day, when I had asked a friend along to help with some translation at the computer shop, he offered her a grape.

'He never offers me a taste,' I asked her to tell him with mock hurt.

'Ah, she can taste the grape but you can taste the woman,' was his response, not knowing ours was a friendship rather than a more carnal relationship.

I buy my bulk wine at the wine co-operative, dispensed from bowsers like those at a petrol station, equipped with nozzles and digital displays that read off the number of litres and the price just like their petrol pump equivalents.

Here the locals come to buy the local red, white or rosé table wine. By any measure it is cheap — $NZ2.00 or so for a litre. And they buy in bulk with great flagons and flasks each holding 50 or more litres. The biggest single purchase I ever saw was just over 900 litres but many would buy hundreds of litres at a time. When filled, the flagons need two people to carry them. I feel silly holding my tiny five-litre jar while surrounded by such serious wine drinkers. It was, however, one of the most frustrating places to shop; you could arrive to be faced with a queue of ten people, each wanting to buy so many hundreds of litres. And, infuriatingly, the wine pump operators insist on filling each container right to the brim. This makes for a slow service as anyone who has waited for a petrol tank to be painstakingly 'topped off' will know. But the wine is good and the lady behind the counter ever-friendly, asking where I came from, where I lived, how long I would be in Italy, even introducing me to other English-speaking foreigners like Lassi, from Finland.

She — like most other people I had regular dealings with — was in total contrast to my bank teller. He is surely one of the surliest, most slovenly and lackadaisical people ever to have embarked on a career in a service industry. He 'serves' behind the counter at the Sinalunga bank where I have an account. Behind him, on a support column, is a sign asking customers not to smoke; he invariably has a half-smoked cigarette in his mouth. He almost never takes it out while he serves you; he doesn't need to as he never says a word. When he does remove it, it is just to flick the ash on the floor. He has the social grace and charm of a polar bear with an abscessed tooth. Like that Arctic animal, he exists in an ice-cold world of his own. He is also invariably dressed in a sloppy checked shirt with jeans — a tie is as obviously alien to him as good service. In any case, I do not think he could summon up the wit or the energy to knot it before coming to work. Sloth-like, he is as slow as a wet week and has an air of total apathy about him; I am surprised he has lived so long as the energy to draw a breath seems beyond him. Even more astonishing is the fact that he retains his job. Perhaps it is a reflection of work-creation Italy. He would certainly never survive in a service industry position in any other country I can imagine. It is as if life has burdened him with, well, life. Mercifully, his compatriots embrace life with gusto rather than his sullen temperament.

And none more so than Franco. I first met Franco in a Hammamet hotel during a winter escape with Nancy to the warmth of Tunisia. We joined a group of other guests one evening. What a mixed bag we were — a young couple from the English Midlands, a rather pompous Frenchman, the effervescent Diane who collected 'my friends' like a philatelist collects stamps, ourselves (a Kiwi and an American) and Franco, the ceramics expert who helped companies establish new factories.

The Frenchman spoke no English and somewhat brusquely repelled my efforts to talk to him in my halting French. He was having an affair with Diane who spoke no French; I suppose the language of love is an international one, but I struggled to imagine post-coital lovers' talk between them.

Diane did, however, speak Italian, having lived in Italy for many years. This helped us converse with the happy-eyed Franco, who spoke no English. He had lived in Cairo for some three years ('very good') before moving to another contract in Saudi Arabia and then on to Tunisia. We discovered that he came from the little crossroads village of Torrienieri, perhaps 25 kilometres from San Clemente. His wife, Isabella, lived there during his foreign assignments, and his daughter owned the only restaurant in the town, a pizzeria. This was the town I passed through each morning on my way to the vendemmia at La Magia on the slopes below Montalcino. Franco said he was returning to Torrienieri in the summer for a holiday and we took his phone number to call him then. I thought at the time that it was another example of how small the world can be, to have discovered an Italian from so close to my new home in a hotel lounge in Tunisia. Two months later I was to find out how very small indeed it actually is.

In April, I flew again to New Jersey and to Nancy. I caught the train to Rome from the ancient Etruscan stronghold of

Chiusi. As I stood in the queue to buy my ticket there was a tap on my shoulder and I heard my name in an Italian accent. Turning, there was the broad-smiling face of Franco. He had been back home to Torrienieri for a ten-day holiday ('I ask for fifteen days but the director tell me only ten. Many, many problems with director.'). He was returning to Tunisia and we travelled together to Rome's central station, where we had a coffee before proceeding to Leonardo da Vinci Airport.

He told me in his much-improved English that he was still living at our Les Orangiers hotel at Hammamet, commuting each day to the factory in Tunis, about an hour's drive. But he was becoming tired of working in Arab countries — 'Arabs no speak with me in factory. Two hundred and fifty Arabs in factory, me only foreigner. Many, many problems.' His contract was due to expire in the summer and he was already investigating new prospects in China or Russia. We agreed that I would call him on his return to Italy.

I lost his phone number along with others on my return to Rome from the States when I left it lying on top of a public telephone at the station (fortunately I had a back-up book at San Clemente) so was not able to telephone him. But later I called by the pizzeria and was able to join him for dinner.

In this way friendships are formed and built. And when you lose your address book, they become lost too. After losing mine in Rome, I lost the only contact reference with Armando, my new-found friend from the vendemmia and an economics student at Siena University. We had exchanged telephone numbers on that last day of the harvest as we sat around our stone table feeling so pleased with ourselves.

I felt hesitant to call him, however. What could he possibly want to have to do with a man twice his age when he was surrounded by students his own age at the University?

Two or three months after the vendemmia, I was in Siena.

As I walked past the monolithic church of San Domenico on to the bridge that would take me out of the historic 'old town', I heard my name called. And sure enough there was Armando. He had just been saying goodbye to his American girlfriend. As well as our vendemmia comradeship, we had a commonality in our love lives. We both had American girlfriends who lived in different places; his taught English in Florence and despite the distance, he at least could see her each weekend while I faced a 24-hour journey to get to my love in Bridgewater, New Jersey, from the time I left San Clemente. Delighted with our chance meeting (and such chance encounters seemed to have become a regular part of my life since my departure from New Zealand), we shook hands warmly. I apologised and explained why I had not telephoned. He told me he had wanted to call but felt his English was too bad! We arranged to meet again and would later spend afternoons in Siena's Irish Pub, one of the 'in' places among the student population.

Armando was in a dilemma. He came from the deep south of Italy, on its heel. His family had spent many thousands of dollars to send him to university here in Siena. But he was a dissatisfied young man. When I met him he had already been scrimping, as student life dictates, for some years. He faced another two or three further years of this existence. Then, he explained, he would have to spend another additional few years getting unpaid work experience, if he could find it. So he would be 30 or older before he could even hope to find a paid job. The prospect of a new life with an American wife in the promised land that drew so many Italian and other migrants over the years seemed a very attractive option to him. And who could blame him? But how to tell his parents, who had put such an investment into the education of their son?

I never found out which life he chose; whatever it was, I wish him well.

CHAPTER SIXTEEN

The Italianisation of Nancy

SHE ARRIVED ONE July day in that first summer. It had been a long wait, more than ten months since we first met in Bath. I admired her courage. She had given up much to get here — a family and friends, a secure job, a good income, corporate share options, a home, a car, a life that allowed her to do what she wanted when she wanted. Now she was entering a totally foreign world.

'That's it! I'm moving to another country!' she stormed.

'Which one,' I asked, curious.

'I don't know. One which has measuring marks on the butter wrapping paper.'

'How will you know if the country has them?'

'I'll call ahead,' she said smugly.

It was to be a rocky introduction. The water pump had already broken on the July day that she arrived to live at San Clemente.

We had a houseful of guests and we were taking bucket baths on the back lawn.

The plum tree was shedding fruit like Molly, the Alsatian, sheds hair and we were struggling to cope with the volume of fruit, reluctant to see any go to waste.

The temperature was off the scale and the sun seared through the window like an acetylene torch through paper. It was a sorry beginning to her new life.

The Italianisation of Nancy, Week Two. Enrico had foolishly let himself run out of lamb chops on the very day that Nancy decided to cook them. Not only that, he had no lamb legs or shoulders either.

'What sort of butcher doesn't have lamb? Anyway, the lambs are so frigging small here. The snake [grass, living in the water pump housing] has bigger shoulders!'

Week Three. The gentle, loving Molly sits outside in the blazing sun for hours, hurt by the (friendly) telling off she had from Nancy for bringing muddy paws into the house. She only went to the frog pond to cool off. What's a little mud on a tile floor out here in the country?

Week Four. 'What's wrong with this frigging fridge? Everything goes off so quickly.' And: 'What is it about Italian bakers? Don't they know about salt? Keeps the bread from going stale and gives it some flavour at least?' And: 'It's no frigging use. I can't cook half these recipes because there's no frigging ingredients in the shops.'

Nancy's initiation into the classroom of Tuscany was mercifully brief. But it was a steep learning curve. And I have to admit that her frustrations were entirely understandable and accurate in those early learning days as she adapted to a new country, new language, new culture and a new way of doing things.

Italy can be a test of patience that would sorely try Job. At any one time, both minor and major mishaps lurk in ambush. As I write now the television is being repaired, we await a replacement part for the dishwasher, the refrigerator door is broken and rapidly coats with ice after defrosting, the chest freezer seal doesn't work effectively, the car is waiting to go into the garage for a 1000-kilometre readjustment after yet again blowing the engine (perhaps the part we have been waiting for for four months will have finally arrived?), the fireplaces send more smoke into the house than up the chimney, the Internet has been 'down' for five of the last nine days, the tape deck needs fixing, the weed-eater needs a new gasket for the petrol tank and the remaining section of the tiled roof in the courtyard buildings could cave in any day. Nancy soon discovered that the 'small' lamb chops — when the butcher had them — were displayed next to delicacies like pigs' ears and tails; Italian shopping hours seemed entirely random; tradesmen were mainly incompetent (you quickly learn to expect anything repaired to break down again within a day or so), and Italian drivers were unpredictable.

She was already familiar with the local area after her three visits so was not walking into an unknown environment. She had also had many months to consider her decision and plan for it, unlike my experience of being flung somewhat sharply into the deep end. So adapt she did and quickly, despite the hiccups of frustration. And as a scientist she brought a welcome and much needed order.

We cleaned and sorted through the kitchen cupboards, unearthing relics like an old mixer and gelato ice cream maker as well as a brand-new blender. We discarded old food that had sat in bottles and jars on the shelves for what appeared to be years. We put a new cover on the wooden kitchen table.

It was a thorough going-over and in the end, Nancy felt

satisfied enough to announce, 'Now I feel comfortable.'

We got a barbecue up and smoking with my cousin Richard. We began a modest garden with plantings of fennel and radishes. We went for walks in the lane picking fruits and berries growing wild. We cooked them, dried them in the sun for winter months or froze them. With our newly uncovered ice cream maker we made blackberry gelato. We had fresh plum tarts. We dried figs on trays under a fine mesh screen in the sun. I made fig preserves; Nancy made blackberry and apple pies. She went on to the Internet to find ways to cure the ripening olives from the trees lining our lane. It was a disaster. We developed a herb garden — chillies, basil, thyme, and chives to compliment the rosemary, sage and lavender lining the driveway and the mint in the old water trough. I plucked grapes from the vines.

We picked up handfuls of chestnuts from the churchyard at Montefollonico, the domes and towers of Montepulciano away on its distant hill. They (the chestnuts) were of the horse variety — mouth-puckering bitter. We tapped pine nuts from the trees, discarding the earwigs that dwelt there too.

At the locals' market in Florence, well off the beaten tourist track, we found fresh ginger for the first time. And we discovered that it *is* possible to barter in Italy. At the second-hand clothes stalls we bargained for a warm winter jacket and a sports coat for me and a smart jacket for Nancy. Both were of high quality and in excellent condition.

Nancy began teaching herself the piano with a book we bought in Somerville, near her old home in Bridgewater. That went on the back burner as we started Italian lessons. We had thought of learning the language at the school for foreigners at Siena University. But the time commitment was excessive — three to four hours a day, five days a week, for three months. We discovered Joe in nearby Petroio, who taught English and German to Italians as well as piano. Typically, in this topsy-turvy new world, he was German! He had been living in Italy for some years. On Wednesday afternoons we would drive to the tiny town, park in the carpark just outside the old city wall and walk up to where he lived, past the terracotta factories, the steeply banked old houses, the ancient cross of the Knights Templar, the forever gushing public water fountain, the cat that liked to sit in the sun at its doorway and the little dog that sometimes escorted us for part of the walk. There we would spend an hour in their tiny kitchen, seated around the table with the shaggy white dog at our feet and one of the cats on Nancy's lap, returning to long-forgotten schooldays of conjugations and past participles.

I sadly became a drop-out. By now I was involved in putting this manuscript together and found it impossible to concentrate. Nancy persisted; this was one of her long-term goals, to learn a foreign language.

We went swimming in the snowmelt-blue, tepid waters of the cliff-bottom pool at Bagno Vignoni. Above us were great outcrops of silica, rippled like a human brain. We daubed our faces with the fine silt from the bottom of the pool and sat in the water while the summer sun caked it dry. Perhaps we would later sit on the smooth stone above the pool, our bottoms in the gentle flow, plucking wild ripe blackberries from the poolside bush.

We found a bar in Sinalunga where we played pool — it had proper balls, good cues, plenty of elbow room and reasonable felt. It gloried in the name Super Pizza Brothers and was the hang-out for Sinalunga's young set, with wall-to-wall video games, cheap pizzas and the ghastly disco music that Italians adore.

We went into hack-and-chop mode as autumn neared. Anything with a limb or leaf was fair game. Victims of our pruning efforts included the rosemary and lavender bushes,

Elario's acacia trees, the holm oak in the back lawn, the mulberry tree, the back fig tree and the solitary rose bush.

We went surfing, too. For recipes, news and research. As our bounty of berries and fruit from nature increased, we sought help from the Internet to help us put it to good use. We found new recipes to try, sometimes with farcical results.

One day Nancy decided she wanted to try the rabbit from Enrico. She surfed her way into an Italian recipe collection and translated it into English on our Internet translation system.

Recipe One. Rabbit to the Olives.

Washed to along the rabbit in running water, sgocciolatelo and tagliatelo to pieces; disponetelo in one casserole of terracotta with the butter and the oil; lasciatelo to rosolare well, you add to the wine white man, salate and pepate. Prepared while made trito of rosmarino, the olives, the pinoli and the prezzemolo. You melt in a lukewarm water bowl the dice and a spoonful of flour white woman and add this compound to the rabbit. Left to cook for approximately half hour and joined trito of aromas and the crushed segments of garlic. Fairies to still cook slowly, for approximately an hour and that is until when the meat very is cooked and the sughetto dense. Accompanied with one smoking polenta, or with crostini of polenta fried in oil.

Recipe Two. Rabbit to the Cipolline.

Fairies to recover in least butter of the pezzetti of ventresca of pig. When they are fried taglieteli and sostituiteli in the casserole with infarinati pieces of rabbit. Fairies to rosolare for approximately five minuteren. White man and means of brodo bathed then with a wine glass. You replace pezzetti of ventresca with a Po of rooms and pepper; left to cook for an hour. While to part sbucciate of the cipolline and fatele to recover in the butter, addolcendole with a pochino of sugar; fairies then to fry in the butter of the crostini of bread. In the capacity plate to repair the cipolline and the crostini, interposing pieces of rabbit with the relative gravy.

On my trips to New Jersey I began trolling through Nancy's food magazines for recipes. She already had some marked favourites and these went into a white folder that I nicknamed *The White Album*. Ones that appealed to me went into my own folder, *The Off-White Album*. There was a large array of recipe magazines and cookbooks at San Clemente but most were in Italian; it took longer to translate a recipe than to cook it.

There were also some English language cookbooks. It was an eclectic assortment of the odd and the downright bizarre. From its ranks I could pluck a book of Swedish cooking, a numbingly banal collection of unappetising and bland recipes like fried pork with brown beans or cabbage soup. I could make reindeer casserole, roast saddle of reindeer or a game casserole of elk or reindeer. This would be interesting to try. Sadly, the woods around me do not have a ready population of elk or reindeer.

Or I could indulge in the mysteries of the East from my collection of Japanese, Chinese and Indian cookbooks. Sadly again, ingredients like mirin, lotus seeds and kalonji seed are not stocked on the shelves alongside the pasta and pomodori of Italy.

The jellied pork brawn wrapped and pressed in tripe that the *Christmas Festive Day Recipes* book proclaims is traditional English Christmas fare since the Middle Ages is not an alluring prospect.

Curiously, there are two books of *Traditional Irish Cookery* in my little library. How many ways are there to cook potatoes? There is a volume of Jewish cookery — rather odd in Catholic Italy.

But perhaps the most bizarre offering in my international collection is a little duck-egg blue covered booklet called simply *Some Icelandic Recipes*. From it I can take recipes for baked cod, steamed cod, fried cod, boiled cod, battered whole cod, fillet of cod. For a change, I can try baked salmon, steamed salmon, fried salmon, boiled salmon, whole salmon, fillet of salmon. It offers me roast leg of lamb, grilled leg of lamb, roast saddle of lamb, fried lamb cutlets, 'The bachelor's leg of lamb', 'The suffragette's leg of lamb', fried London lamb, broiled London lamb, melon with London lamb, salt lamb and yellow pea soup, lamb soup, spiced lamb meatroll, fried lamb meatroll, lamb pâté, boiled smoked lamb, smoked lamb salad. There is not, unfortunately, a recipe for lamb Christmas cake. Coming from a country known for its sheep I am awed by this miracle of Icelandic culinary inventiveness.

Daunted by this wonderful range of gourmet opportunities, Nancy and I resorted to our albums. We even set up *The Cream Album*, where we stored recipes that we both tried and liked, our 'keepers'.

Fittingly, in a country that devotes so much time and enthusiasm to the fine art of eating, our evenings revolved around the kitchen table. Lunches and breakfasts were a less rigid affair, each eating what and when we liked. But the evening meal became an important part of the day.

We took daily turns at cooking. Typically, meal preparation would begin in the early evening. While one of us prepared the meal, the other would sit at the table. We drank wine and chatted. It might take three or four hours to prepare, cook and eat our dinner. They became special times. When visitors came to stay or guests came to dinner, we would all sit around the table rather than gather in the lounge. It was a big old farmhouse-style kitchen and was a comforting, welcoming and warm environment that everyone enjoyed. From our recipe albums came delights like roast pepper and orange soup, potatoes with asparagus, peas and arugula, pork escallopes with marsala wine and apples, Garfunkel chicken (parsley, sage, rosemary and thyme), whole roast chicken stuffed with lemon and herbs, barbecued pork with honey, mustard and rosemary.

Some foods we introduced to each other. These were written into the coffee-table *Couples* book that Nancy had bought for us in New Jersey. As well as new foods, other aspects of our life together went into the book. What attracted us to each other, our first date, photos in Oxford and Siena, why we'll always remember our first kiss (Nancy: 'I stood quite rigid because I was afraid my knees would give way'), things we gave each other, our differences and similarities, our best personality and physical attributes and the best and worse of times.

We kept the book on the lounge coffee table for guests to leaf through if they were interested.

We also began a list of things we would each like to do or achieve before we died. Like our recipe book library, it was an eclectic collection. Allan: to fly in the Concorde, to see an opening or closing ceremony at the Olympic Games, to go up the Amazon, to travel around the US in a campervan for two years, to spend a barbecue afternoon with American columnist and funny man Dave Barry. Nancy: to own a sports car, to visit New Zealand, to go to an Eric Clapton concert in a small theatre, to live in a house overlooking the ocean, to meet Robert de Niro ('he's so intense'), Mel Gibson ('he seems just so much fun') and Kevin Costner ('he seems such a nice, ordinary guy').

Pipe dreams all, perhaps. Maybe in some distant year or another life we may achieve one or two of them; the fun is really in imagining them. But for the moment it was time for Nancy to settle into her new country and new home — to 'go Italian'. That in itself was challenge enough.

CHAPTER SEVENTEEN

Foot Scraping, Foot Baths and Face Packs

THE FOOT SCRAPER certainly knew his place. And his business.

He sat downstream from the rest of us as we soothed and massaged our feet in the gentle warmth of the mineral stream.

He had come well prepared for a self-conducted, self-indulgent pedicure session in the sunshine on the cliff that overlooks the Orcia River in southern Tuscany. As his feet softened in the foot-wide trench that carried the waters to the cliff face just beyond him, he began scraping and scouring at the pads of his soles, removing calloused skin from a lifetime of work to be swept away down the crystallised face of the 50-metre high cliff. For this task he allowed some fifteen or twenty minutes. Then, satisfied, he turned to the scissors and spent an unhurried fifteen minutes clipping and cleaning his toe nails. Again, the 'tailings' were swept away.

Comfortable at last, he carefully towelled each foot, replaced his shoes and socks, unrolled his trouser legs, replaced his jacket and walked away until another day at Bagno Vignoni. The other locals a few metres upstream from us continued happily doing their knitting, drinking their flasked coffee, reading their books, chatting with friends or just sitting back and enjoying the luxury of the best free foot bath you could hope to find.

The Bagno Vignoni thermal waters are among Italy's most famed. The indisposed come from around the world to 'take the waters' in the hope of curing ailments like arthritis and rheumatism, just as they have come since the long-vanished age of the Etruscans. The mix of minerals such as sulphur, carbon and calcium that spring from the earth at a constant slipper-warm temperature have been heralded through more than two millennia. Evidence of people's search for succour still exists in the vast thermal pool that serves as the spa's *piazza*, closed for bathing but with plans to reopen it.

In the resort hotel, earnest German tourists don the mandatory rubber swim caps and cavort in the open-air pool, complete with attentive staff at the bar and a low-slung diving board for those particularly heady moments of gaiety. The setting is superb, the history ancient, the waters sublime. But the pool is a jarring note, more in keeping with a lido at an upmarket resort than the serene, calming, invigorating experience that a mineral spa should offer those who come for whatever need they have.

So Nancy and I ignore the jostling, jumping Germans and join the locals — the foot scraper, the knitters, the readers, the town gossips. The path to the cliff top that overlooks the river is cut down one side by a narrow stream, descending in a series of small, ankle-deep pools. This is where the locals hang out. They come to sit on the side of the stream and rest their feet in the pools of warm mineral water overflowing from the pool in the *piazza* as it flows towards the cliff top. We sit downstream from the socialisers but upstream from the foot scraper, who has chosen his position near the cliff face to avoid offending others.

The water is miraculous; the minerals set up such a sensuous feeling of comfort seeping through the skin so deeply that your whole body is warmed by them. It is a glorious sensation, enhanced by the sun, the steeply rising hills across the river floor and the ambience reaching out from your fellow foot bathers.

After a time, the Italian woman sitting alongside us, a pool or two upstream, dries her feet and leaves. As she does so, she indicates that we should move to her pool, which is deeper. It is a kindly gesture towards obvious strangers (and foreigners at that) and one which we appreciate and respond to gladly.

In the sun the rich colours of accumulated salts and algae glisten — reds and greens and browns. They are the visible evidence of the healing and life that these waters have promised over these past centuries. The 'hard' minerals carried by the spring water from deep below the surface of the earth are also on show as huge clumps and clouds and nodules of crystals that tumble down the face of the cliff like the water itself. And down below, too, is a promise for the summer. A large pool of glacier-melt white sits tepidly in the chill shadow of the cliff before finding its only outlet through a small channel that runs to the river.

In the high heat of a Tuscan July and August, it does become an idyllic destination — an oasis in the midst of the rainless countryside that has become our home. We drive to the town and turn onto the bumpy dirt road that takes us down towards the pool. We park the car and shielded by its open doors change into our swimming gear, then walk down the road to a 20-metre high climb over ages-old grey mineral deposits, worn smooth by the countless pairs of feet that have made the same journey since the springs above and the pool were first discovered — by whom? Ancient cave dwellers? We emerge onto a small plateau that is almost entirely made up of the pool — about 50 metres long and six metres wide. If we are lucky — and to enhance our luck we time our visits for the mid-week Italian lunch hour when most locals and visitors to the spas above are at table — the pool is usually all but deserted. We leave our towels and sandals beside the small path that fringes one side and walk in from the easiest access at one end. The water is only thigh deep at most and as we proceed further, the fine, soft, milky-white mineral silt that covers the bottom is kicked up to the surface in swirling clouds by our feet.

The water is barely tepid, cooled during its descent from the stream above. But in high summer's searing heat, it is glorious.

We swim a little (breast stroke is about the only proper swimming stroke achievable), float and propel ourselves backwards with outstretched arms, sit with our backs against the smoothed pool walls and stand with our backs or tummies against the worn surface where the water spills on its final metre or so into the pool — the temperature warmer than the pool water.

We daub our faces, necks and shoulders with the silt mud from the bottom, scooping up handfuls to smear over us. Then we sit white-faced as if with a death mask, our faces to the sun while it dries before rinsing it off. It is a rustic face pack with all the therapeutic goodness that people pay thousands of dollars for at health spas around the world.

Later, we might sunbathe on the mineral rocks, or on the pool side with legs dangling in the water or, at one end, in little pools where the water runs across a gently sloping, flat surface of rock into the pool. We pick wild blackberries from the bushes that grow at the edge. Or we might take a picnic lunch and bottle of chilled white wine to eat and drink beside the river.

'This is paradise,' says Nancy one day. And she's right.

But even before summer's heated arrival, before autumn has ended, we return to the foot bathing trench of Bagno Vignoni on a clear, sunny, still and warm mid-November morning. What leaves remain are now brown with death and blow into the water that steams in the autumn air. As they flow past, they brush your ankles. We are the only ones there this time, at least for half an hour, and we reflect how lucky we are. Later, a group of four young people — German tourists, we guess — walk by us to look over the cliff face. Confident with the 'way' we have shown them, they, too, remove their boots, their socks, roll up their jeans legs and plunge in up to their ankles. Soon they are lost in a world that encompasses only them. But this narrow, short stream encourages, even demands such a response. It is a communal, public environment where the participants can none the less enter their own private domain.

It is a place for lovers to share secret smiles and open hearts.

As Nancy says, 'It's like you're walking on clouds.'

CHAPTER EIGHTEEN

And So To Be Wed . . .

I FORGOT THE rings. The limo driver got a ticket. My best men wore earrings and high heels. The brides were kept waiting . . .

By any reckoning, it was a memorable occasion — a year to the day that we first met in Bath. Considering I had not wanted a love relationship before meeting Nancy, it was a curious way to end my first year in Tuscany.

It happened one warm August evening in the Christ Episcopal Church of Middletown, New Jersey. Like any wedding, planning had been underway for months. Nancy resolutely refused to divulge the secrets of her wedding dress.

'You're not going to see it until I come down that aisle. It's simple but elegant. That's as much as you'll get.'

By August, she had already been living at San Clemente for some four weeks, so we flew together from Rome to Newark, arriving a week before the big day. We needed that time — tuxedo fittings, shoe buying, catching up with her friends, buying candles, getting our Red Cross provisions to take back to Italy (books, herbs, pen refills, writing pads, clothes . . . the type of item that was either not available or outrageously expensive there). The wedding licence was a particularly important document to collect.

We also visited the editor of the local *Middletown Courier*. I had felt the circumstances surrounding the wedding — a double ceremony, Nancy moving to Tuscany, a local family — were sufficiently interesting to warrant an article in it. Unbeknown to Nancy's family, I wrote a piece and took it to the editor. It duly appeared on the eve of the ceremony and everyone seemed quite pleased.

The rehearsal was the night before. It was the first double wedding for our Minister, Ellen, and she was determined that it was not going to be 'a circus' if she had anything to do with it. It certainly had that potential! Ellen was a treasure, a warm, gracious, gentle, smiling and caring person. She offered some words of wisdom as the rehearsal finished: 'Don't worry if things go wrong. Those are the things that you remember about your wedding, not when nothing happens.'

The big day got under way with me being bundled out of the house. There was no way I was going to be around to see that dress before it came down the aisle! I took my wedding suit and our overnight bag to the hotel where we were to stay after the reception. There, later in the morning, Jean and Karen picked me up and we went to a nearby town for lunch. I had asked them to be my 'best people', or witnesses, as we had become good friends. None of my New Zealand family or friends could afford the cost or the time of the journey to New Jersey.

We went to a restaurant with an attached cigar club, one of those curious American institutions where cigar smokers gather to enjoy a smoke and a chat. We finished our meals with port and cigars. It was a very mellowing way to get through a good part of the day. I sat regally in the rear seat of the cherry red Ford Mustang convertible that they had borrowed for the outing.

After lunch, they dropped me back at the hotel to get dressed while they went home to do the same. They were to return at 5 pm, when the hired stretched limo was also due to arrive to take us to the church in good time and then pick up Nancy and Sue, her Maid of Honour. We had plenty of time. Hah!

Everything at the hotel was going to plan. The hotel reception staff had taken photos. The limo had arrived and we were enjoying a nerve-soothing beer on the way to the church.

'So now's probably a good time to give us the rings,' said Karen.

I surprised myself with the calm note in my voice.

'I don't have them.'

'You don't?'

'No, they're back at the hotel.'

My sangfroid masked a churning stomach and knife-edged nerves as we waited to get off the freeway and return to the hotel to pick up the rings I had left in the wardrobe. The limo driver couldn't believe it. 'Has this ever happened to you before?' I asked her. 'No, never!' Great.

She tried to make up time with an illegal turn. Sure enough, there was a cop behind her and we had to sit in the car while he wrote her a ticket. He was one of those young macho guys who wear sunglasses, a uniform and a pistol to show the world how tough they are. He could see we were a wedding party but still insisted on writing the ticket. I wanted to talk to him, explain what had happened. But Jean just told me to shut up — she was worried about explaining to Nancy how her husband-to-be was in the local jail instead of saying, 'I do.'

By the time we got the ticket, got the rings and got through the now heavy rush-hour traffic, we were nearly 30 minutes late getting to the church. I leapt out of the car and apologised to everyone I could see. Patti was outside with her party. Nancy and Sue were still sitting in the limo — there was no way I was going to see that dress!

We hurried round the church to go in by a side door. Poor Mike was a bundle of nerves — he had been there for two hours by this stage.

Finally we were able to get my buttonhole flower on and we marched into my marriage.

The dress — and Nancy — were simply beautiful. Her face beamed as her Mum and Dad led her down the aisle. I don't think she stopped smiling for the next six or seven hours.

Richie and Mary then wheeled back down the side wall of the church to escort Patti to Mike. In this way we were finally able to get the ceremony started. From there, the rest of the day went predictably. Nancy's and Patti's brother-in-law, Joe, gave a reading. Her friend Joni read a poem I had written for Nancy in April. And of course we exchanged vows. Ellen had urged us to remember them and we ensured later that we would by taping them to the refrigerator door in the kitchen at San Clemente.

We lit candles for each other and for my two sons back in New Zealand. Jean, ever practical, carried tissues in her tuxedo jacket pockets. We said, 'I do.' And so, a year almost to the hour that Nancy and I met in Bath, we became husband and wife. It felt pretty damned good.

Photographs, greetings and well-wishing finally completed, the two bridal parties went to their separate limos for the drive to the reception. We five opened a bottle of chilled Perriet Jouet (I hadn't forgotten that!), yahooed, photographed each other and generally agreed that we were the best-looking bridal party in the history of the world. The business of the rings and the ticket we put down to pre-wedding nerves. Just as we did the fact that Nancy forgot to shampoo her hair before putting conditioner on and had to double back for the forgotten veil on the way to the hairdressers.

As we arrived at the reception, I was amazed to be called to the desk for a telephone call. It was my old and dear friend Terry, ringing from New Zealand. While I was talking to him I had to take a second call, from another great friend, Rhonda. So there I was with two telephones, trying to conduct a three-way conversation.

The evening of the reception raced by in a blur of dancing, posing for cameras, greeting people, smoking cigars and speeches. The next day my new friends Stan and Suzanne joined us for a day at Sandy Hook National Park on the Jersey shore. I had first met them in June, in the butcher's at Trequanda; they were holidaying at the tourist apartment complex at nearby Montelifre. We exchanged meals and I took them one day on my now-established tour of the towns. We stayed in touch and they drove from Vermont for the wedding.

They were my special guests and I wanted to spend some time with them and introduce Nancy. Our day out at the beach was a grand opportunity as they stayed overnight. Stan was both amused and bemused to share the first day of the honeymoon with the bride and groom. 'We've been to more than a hundred weddings and this has never happened before,' he said as we sipped cold beers, ate store-bought sandwiches and lazed in the hot August sun with the ever-impressive Manhattan skyline in the background.

Nor had it happened to me.

CHAPTER NINETEEN

A Feast of Funghi

AT THE END of my first year at San Clemente and the beginning of Nancy's, we enjoy yet another sensation from the larder that nature shares with us — the gloriously rich taste of freshly gathered wild mushrooms.

It is the last of the many food joys we have picked and plucked in these last eight weeks or so — blackberries, grapes, figs, fresh herbs, plums — but our wild funghi seems the best of all for their strength of flavour that simply cannot be matched by the efforts of mushroom farmers.

Only the wine grapes and the olives remain of the major crops now before the land settles down for its winter sleep. But in the coming weeks, we will reap our own harvest along the lane, in the yard and through the woods.

We might start our evening meal with a quickly sautéed pan of funghi we picked that morning, finished with a *panna funghi* (a new addition to the Co-op — heavy cream laced with porcini mushrooms), a dash of Marsala and a sprinkling of fresh thyme from the pot in the courtyard. Or it may be a mid-morning brunch — omelette filled with wild mushrooms we picked just moments before and sprinkled with freshly chopped parsley.

'That had the most flavour of any mushroom omelette I've ever tasted — or any omelette at all for that matter,' said a satisfied Nancy after I cooked the first one.

We quickly developed a morning ritual — coffee, perhaps some breakfast and then, armed with bowl and knife and the ever present Molly, we stroll out to harvest the overnight crop.

These are outings that bring back special memories for each of us. For me, it is the memory of a city boy on a farm holiday in a New Zealand autumn, wandering the dewy early morning pastures and returning with a bucket load to have for breakfast, or perhaps a rich farmhouse mushroom soup that night as the tiredness of a country day crept over me.

The beauty of the land around us is enough to satisfy any hunger some mornings. The mist still hovers in the woods and valleys and fields as we set out. The bare, ploughed fields seem like a lunar landscape or desert dunes rough with stone. Only the tops of the trees in the woods are visible as the mist courses through their limbs, stirred by the warming sun. A lone tree in the field stands eerily silent, as still as the air itself.

The dew now sits heavily on the grass, but it is still too early for frosts. And in the morning sun the droplets set thousands of spiders' webs glistening — draped through the branches of shrubs, strung between the fence wire, stretched across the ground itself and even slung from one side of the lane to the other — a feat of engineering and acrobatic skill that amazes me.

Each morning as we set out, the sun-bathing frogs on the side of the cattle pond in the field outside San Clemente 'plop', 'plop', 'plop' as they high-dive into the pond, providing a comical start to our outing. Sometimes I find a nomadic toad on the back lawn and take him back to his friends.

On some mornings I pick a small bunch of the white or red grapes hanging in clusters from the vines at the entrance to the apartment block down the lane. The owners have gone for the year and the grapes just wither on the vine, so I feel no guilt about helping myself. Nancy does not like them — 'the skins are too tough and there are too many seeds' — but I find them sweet and juicy. It is a very sensual feeling — walking along a Tuscan country lane searching for wild mushrooms and eating my breakfast straight from the vine. The drying juice from the fruit becomes sticky on my fingers by the time we get back to the house.

As we walk through the woods and along the lane, the sun turns the air a golden green as it hits the now-turning leaves of the trees and dapples the ground around us. But of course we are on a mission — to find, fetch and feast on earth-sprung delights. And we do not lack for choice, even if, in these early autumn days, the pickings are still relatively sparse.

The variety we find in just a short walk to the old abbey below us is astounding. There are the traditional field mushrooms that I remember so well from my New Zealand days. There are the Italian porcini — think-stemmed but not yet as big as they will become. There are the delicate chanterelles, oyster-white and half-trumpet shaped. Finding these presumably French funghi along a Tuscan country lane impresses not only Nancy but also a friend, Viola, who muses, 'Ah, a chanterelle omelette! Wonderful!'

All these we can readily identify. But there are many varieties that remain mysterious and alien to us. 'That's OK to eat,' says Viola, as I show her a large, fleshy red-skinned mushroom with yellow veins and stem. 'I don't like them but people eat them. Many people peel the skin off first because it has a bitter taste.'

There is the tiny frail translucent mushroom that, when the

sun shines through it, turns into a perfect spider's web. It is so fragile that you feel it would simply dissolve away in a sauté pan, perhaps leaving only a webbed shadow on the pan base as a reminder of its existence.

There are the elegant, brown-skinned funghi, their slender white stems crowned with a perfect dome.

Then there are the bizarre and downright nasty-looking types. One large variety has a bright yellow stem that turns deep blue where the stainless steel knife cuts across it. Chillingly, another turns blood red. One morning, in the lane below San Clemente, we come across a crop of big dark brown funghi that look like dog droppings. They have no cap or crown, just a thick stem that has bulldozed its way up through the packed metal surface of the roadway.

'I don't care what anyone says, I'm not eating something that looks like that,' vows Nancy. I agree — these things are not only the power-pushers of the funghus world but probably the meanest-looking food-type I've ever seen. I also discover tucked under an overhanging branch two of the biggest and ugliest mushrooms yet encountered. They are a very deep brown, with white stem and spongy flesh. They are perhaps 20 centimetres wide and resemble cow pats. No, we won't be eating those.

So we remain in wary ignorance about these weird life forms that surround us. Nancy searches the Internet to try to identify ones that will a) kill us, or b) send us off on some mystical mental journey.

'There's this one site that tells you all about the magic mushrooms. It comes with a warning, "You should not eat these, they are illegal," but then has pictures of what each one looks like and what it will do to you. This one will give you euphoria, this one will give you paranoia. I mean the Government health warning is there but then they say, "Well as long as you don't ingest more than ten of these, they won't kill you,"' Nancy reports. 'Ten will kill you but less will give you a great high.'

Then there's the 'Funghus of the Month' site by a mycologist whose latest essay is about the *boletus edulis*, or porcini. It comes with colour photographs but, as Web wanderers will know, close-up shots of plants, flowers, shrubs, insects and porcini mushrooms do not reproduce well on anything but the most expensive of printers.

So in our early days, we remained like the target of our searching — in the dark about the edibility or otherwise of most of our finds. Our caution about the unidentified funghi was also matched by the wariness we often felt just walking off the property and into the lane. For we shared our walks with other creatures. One morning, Nancy leapt back with a cry, 'Oh, a snake!' There in a pool of sunlight at the base of a tree lay a grass snake curled up, perhaps catching a late tan before winter. His gold and green colouring seemed to shimmer metallically in the morning glow. Beautiful and harmless, yes, but a startling encounter just the same.

And then there are the hunters and their dogs, roaming the fields and woods with their fingers locked on their triggers and seemingly ready to blaze away at anything that moves within their peripheral vision. We are very conscious that we are both moving and can easily walk into their range. One morning as we proceeded up the lane some five cars came gingerly past us on our rocky road, all filled with hunters and their dogs.

'What is this? Grand Central Station?' was Nancy's reaction, affronted by the invasion of her territory.

We both instinctively know where the 'primo' spots are to find the funghi. In these early days, they emerge along the roadside at the base of the lane's banks at the top or bottom of the rise that the roadway follows. The young field mushrooms are the easiest to spot — bright white caps and stalks with beautiful salmon veins underneath. Most are elusive, hidden behind overhanging broom or branches, blending in with the foliage or camouflaged by the leaves that are now falling from the trees. We learn to scrape the leaves gingerly from the ground in the likely looking places that are damp, dank, mossy and dark. These are the pockets that smell musty and fecund, ideal for funghi. And we learn where the different types can be found — each variety has its own 'patch' and this is where we know to look. The big, brown-veined field mushrooms grow in a small patch no bigger than a half-metre square by the roadside just 50 metres from the villa. The fresh-white champignons with the salmon pink flesh choose the road verge itself and, as the rains and cold deepen, start springing up in a nearby stretch of low grass. The elegant little chanterelles have a colony along the bank of the lane which is mossy, moist and dark. 'The chanterelle capital of the world,' exclaims Nancy. And, later, 'The porcini capital of the world.' And then, 'The field mushroom capital of the world!' We are careful to cut the stems with a sharp knife leaving the roots in the ground for, hopefully, next autumn's harvest.

With our knowledge and cunning, our daily harvest increases to about a soupbowl full, enough to keep us satisfied and keen to continue our daily forays. And each day we discover new varieties about which we know nothing. We feel very frustrated having this bounty at our doorsteps but not knowing if it is safe to eat.

Viola offers us the solution. We can pick those varieties we do not know and take them to the *farmacia* on the road leading from Sinalunga's railway station to the old central *piazza* high above the spreading town.

'They will tell you what is good and what is not. And in October there is a funghi fair in the school where you can take them,' she tells us.

So we bring home these freaks of funghi nature and store them in the fridge to take them to the *farmacia*. We will also find out the dates of the funghi fair. Like schoolchildren taking a home science project to class, we fill a bowl with our specimens and head to Sinalunga for teacher inspection. 'Teacher' is the very affable, 30-something Dr Cesare. His dispensing room is at the rear of the pharmacy shop and displays two large posters, each with about 30-40 photos of various mushroom types. One poster illustrates edible funghi, the other inedible. Ominously, two of the inedible photos have had the word 'MORTALE' printed under them by hand in large black, very important capital letters.

Collectively, the colours and shapes looked like the drawings of mushrooms and toadstools you find in a children's picture book or a scene on the back lawn of a garden with plaster gnomes fishing from them or even those bouncy creations in the kiddie's playground at a McDonald's outlet.

The posters obviously showed the most common varieties because Cesare hauled a large stack of books from a cupboard to help him identify the seven or eight different specimens we had brought with us. One by one he examined the colour, the stems, the flesh . . . and one, by one, he told us, 'Non buon,' no good. One or two, we were confident, were the prized porcini. Yes, he said, they were from the same *boletus* family that the porcini come from, but, alas, ours were still 'non buon'.

Our last offering was, at least, of some interest. Cesare — later to become 'Dr C' to Nancy — took one look at the delicate brown funghi with the perfect pixie cap and began a description of its family and characteristics. Amidst his explanation one word shrieked out at me, *allucinazione*. Even with my still limited Italian, it was obvious that we had discovered magic mushrooms on our patch at San Clemente! It was a fun notion but we do not even have to talk to understand that we will avoid not only the magic variety, but all funghi we find except the easily-recognisable field mushroom and chanterelles.

But on our way back home, we stop at the fruit and vegetable stall and buy two cultivated porcini to inspect them more thoroughly in the hope we will find them in our woods and fields. Hope springs eternal! It certainly does at the chanterelle capital of the world where each day we hope to find our little white forest of chanterelle seedlings grown to logging size. Each day, stubbornly, they show little sign of growth. And then one day we stumble on a real treasure — big white trumpet-shaped funghi that we spot from the jeep as we drive up the lane towards our Trequanda road. We are convinced it is the mother of all chanterelles. Just metres from this find is another snow-pure mushroom shaped like the cultivated mushrooms you find in supermarkets, but about ten times larger and fatter. We have seen a cluster of these on our daily walks down the lane and had determined to take them, with some other 'X-factor' varieties we found, to the good Dr C.

This way of gathering mushrooms — drive-by harvesting — is a novelty for both of us. 'You just take out the car when you want some funghi,' said Nancy delightedly.

Once again, we take our bowl of specimens into Sinalunga for teacher's report.

We proudly pluck our 'chanterelle', expecting a big smile and hearty congratulations from Dr C. Alas, 'non buon'!

But our 'big buttons', as Nancy decided to call them, are 'buon' — with a very definite caveat. He points to the wall poster that shows the inedible varieties. Alarmingly, he indicates that our big button is from the same family as one of the most prominently displayed funghi on the poster — one of those with the hand-written 'MORTALE' under it.

Dr C shows us how to tell the difference. We listen very carefully. This could literally be a life-or-death decision out in the field. If the part of the stem that grows in the ground is yellow, 'non buon'. But if it is white it is 'va bene', OK. Another indicator is the floury-like dusting where the cap separates from the stem as it grows out. The presence of this substance, like flour doused in oil, is another sign that we can eat and survive. These are important lessons from our good teacher who seemed delighted to see us again. Perhaps we became his science project — educating the *stranieri* into the complex world of funghi.

Such is the variety that greets us daily that ever increasingly we resort to the Internet. Nancy discovers a treatise titled 'A few good mushrooms' by two Slovenians named Miso and Joh, complete with colour photographs.

'Well Slovenia is in this part of the world so what they have there we should have here, right?' she explains when I raise my eyebrows at her source.

From the (English language) print-out we learn of some 25 edible varieties. They revel in their Slovenian and scientific titles. The prized porcini rises majestically to Slovenian life as *Jesenski goban*. It is, Miso and Joh assure us, one of the safest mushrooms because 'it can be easily distinguished from poisonous ones'! (My emphasis.) Exactly how is not explained.

'The most dangerous look-alikes are *Vrazji goban* and *Heponigi goban*: both have reddish and yellowish stems [while the stipe — presumably stem to non-mycologists — of the safe variety is white], but, more importantly, both will turn first dark blue, then black where cut or bruised.' This has a very familiar ring to us.

Miso and Joh seem, in fact, to delight in alerting us to the poisonous look-alikes as much as the 'few good mushrooms'. (I must be fair; their treatise is liberally garnished with warnings that it should not be regarded as a definitive guide. They are seriously into funghi and seriously into the perils.)

Another delicacy of the *boletus* porcini family 'is, however a very tricky mushroom', very similar to those nasty poisonous ones that change colour when you cut them. 'Experts can tell the difference by carmine red scales on the stipe of the *Zametni goban*, while both of the poisonous look-alikes have either a smooth stem (though also carmine red) or a net-like pattern — but I would not bet my life on these details.' Nor will we! And how could one possibly pick from this description?

And so Miso and Joh happily continue playing their Slovenian equivalent of Russian roulette — the game where you keep trying the mushroom and hope you'll live to play again after each pull of the frying-pan trigger.

One, we discover, is 'regarded as the best of all edible mushrooms found in Slovenia. Unfortunately, the deadly *Rdeca musnica* can be mistaken for it with disastrous consequences'! (My emphasis again.)

And the *Travini ski kukmak* (*agaricus campester*) can be 'quite similar' to two of the most poisonous mushrooms around.

Even the most unmushroom-looking morel, famous around the world as a delicacy, has its Darth Vader counterpart. 'The *Pomladanski smreck* is very poisonous.'

To confuse things further, there is a variety that with its intensely-black colouring looks poisonous but is not — 'and there are none even remotely similar'.

So here are the choices we have:

1. Pick those we think are safe but may, in fact, be deadly.
2. Pick those that look poisonous but may, in fact, be fine.
3. Stick to our tried and true field mushrooms and chanterelles.
4. Just buy from the shops — they, presumably, are not eager to poison their customers.

In this dangerous funghi world, where even the names sound

toxic, we decide to stick to the tried and true and if tempted by the more exotic-looking, find them in the market. We do, after all, have much of Tuscany and of Italy — and of the world — yet to see. But we continue our daily outings, returning with enough field mushrooms to give us the glorious taste sensation of autumn and moments we will remember for many years.

CHAPTER TWENTY

Culture: Reflections from a Petri Dish

CULTURE IS AN accumulation of self-interest that defines what a people does and thinks, how it reacts to perceived danger and promise, how it *lives*. It resists the threat of change. It is comfortable with its past and, because of this, its present and future. A culture simmers slowly to life; it does not sizzle. Gradually, over my first year at San Clemente, I discovered more and more about the culture of my hosts.

They epitomise the conservative nature of cultures. They resist, perhaps fear, change. 'We don't like to go outside Italy, we stay close to home and holiday here,' said my Siena student friend Armando. 'Italian girls just want to get married, have babies and live near their mamas. I want to travel, that's why I have an American girlfriend.'

The family is all in Italy. The evidence is everywhere: a grandmother walking out with her granddaughter while her daughter, the child's mother, works; the intense joy and attention people shower on toddlers, the family group at the swings in the park, the extended family gatherings at restaurants (social events as much as a meal); the bond of the *contrada*. The *omerta* of the Cosa Nostra 'family' is a less savoury example, but it does demonstrate the need for acceptance and the notion of strength through unity.

The close-knit sense of family flows into its private territory. The family home is sacred, an island of seclusion like some private chapel on a great baronial English estate. Its walls protect it, comfort it and bind it. The home is for family; the restaurants and bars, nightclubs and dance halls for friends and social outings. Most expatriates I met in my first year confirmed that even after living among Italians and making Italian friends for a dozen or more years, invitations into their homes were rare indeed.

I counted myself lucky to get a glimpse of Italian life on the day I talked to Elario about the war years in his Castelmuzio house. Proud photographs of his life made history books of his walls and cabinets. His new bride Eva showed us their wedding album. The house was a tidy, neat, cosy nest filled with treasures gathered over the decades. We sat at the dining room table and looked out on a splendid view of his grape-vines and olive trees on the slopes of the steep gully opposite. His basement was an eclectic collection of tools, cut-up firewood salvaged from the deadly winter earlier in the decade and great flasks on benches where he stored his harvests of oil and wine.

Elario busied himself in the kitchen, ferrying golden slabs of bruschetta soaked in his oil and coated with so much garlic it seared the throat. Eva kept plying us with delicious sweet cakes and biscuits. As we left, Eva handed Nancy an obviously prized English language biography of Hitler, perhaps her way of remembering the Nazi tyranny in her native Poland. Elario insisted I take a faded copy of the *London Observer* magazine, 30 years old, to help me with my researches into his life in

London after he left his boyhood *mezzadria* at San Clemente behind. It is permanently opened at a feature article on the publisher George Weidenfeld, for whom Elario worked for many years.

These were kind, thoughtful and generous offerings and we treated them with the respect they deserved. They confirmed yet again the generosity I found in so many places and so many ways. The opera-whistling cabinetmaker who repaired an old window frame I found to use as a mount for the Tuscan sunflower print I took to Nancy on our first Christmas. He dismissed me with a wave of his arm when I offered to pay. Tradesmen would tinker and fuss over broken appliances and gadgets and return them to me, again no payment required, thank you, *signore*.

This generosity is matched by the honesty I found in the small towns around me where cars are left unlocked, purses unguarded, valuable new purchases deposited outside shop doors.

This honesty can find its way into the bigger population centres. One day I sat at an outside café in Siena while visitors explored the beauty of the Duomo. I had my back to the patio railing and there was a drop of a metre or so to the street behind me. Turning at a tap on my shoulder, I was handed my wallet that had slipped from my trouser pocket. In most cities in the world, my cash, credit cards, driver's licence, cheque-book and authority to stay at San Clemente would have vanished down a back alley.

The concept of queueing is as far removed from the Italian mind as the concept of Marmite, the tart beef extract that every child in New Zealand grows up with in sandwiches, or the peanut butter and jelly sandwiches of Nancy's childhood. Grocery shops, cafés, hospital waiting rooms, post offices, bank counters . . . to the uninitiated they are a hopeless tangle of customers spread all around and along the available space. They seem at first a crazy free-for-all in which the best elbow-jabber, umbrella-poker and ankle-kicker gets the prize — first place at the counter. It must be hellish for those most steadfast and earnest queuers — the English — when they meet it for the first time. My initial encounter with the teller-from-hell at my Sinalunga bank was an alarming one. Italians gathered around me at the counter like the wasps on the lawn in summer, swarming, humming and *close*. As I wrote out a cheque for cash, eyes watched every digit I filled out. They homed in on my balance. They counted out every 50,000 lire as it was placed before me on the counter. Coming from a culture where customers wait respectfully in line to preserve a monetary privacy, it felt like financial rape. But beneath the apparent turmoil, there is — as always in Italy — a strict order. It is no land-rush happenchance. The Italian sense of rightness is there; there is a queueing system, it just doesn't form itself in a line. Everyone knows exactly when it is their turn to be served. There is a trick to it. You discount everyone who is in the place when you enter. You concentrate only on the people who come in after you. In this way, you know that when it is only those who have followed you that are left, logically you are first in line. It is a subtle, unspoken language, but one that everyone knows, speaks silently and accepts. It has an elegance to it and speaks loudly of the nature of the Italian psyche — a surface irrationality buttressed by a deep current of conservatism, order and the proper way of doing things.

The modest toothpick describes the dichotomy of Italy perfectly. Nicely presented in a transparent plastic container with neatly fitted lid, such toothpicks are elegance itself. The wood is rubbed smooth like a river stone. The 'blunt' end is grooved lovingly. But try to use it for its intended purpose and its soft point folds limply at the touch of your teeth.

Image, presentation, flair, packaging, panache; style versus substance. This is the battlefield of the Italian spirit. If substance can be achieved, excellent. If not, no matter — the design's the thing. It doesn't have to work as long as it looks good not working.

Italy has, of course, a rich heritage of design skill — the great fashion houses of Milan, the world-famous marques of Ferrari and Maserati, the glorious opera houses. To the casual observer, Italy presents a beautiful face. The people dress stylishly, even impeccably. Visitors often comment on the fact. Rarely do you see an ill-dressed or unkempt Italian. Second-hand clothes are also a rarity; at the few market stalls where they are available even these are of high quality — soft leather jackets, cashmere wool overcoats, elegant evening wear.

But at the first chill of winter, the fur coats emerge by the thousand. Every woman in Italy, it seems, has one. How many species have been taken to the brink of extinction by the absolute need to sport a fur coat in the markets of Italy, I wonder, as I see the parade march elegantly by. It seems an indulgence that conveniently ignores the decimation of other creatures that share our world.

Packaging design too is excellent. It is strong, imaginative and stylish. The quality of the contents is almost a secondary concern. Grappa, the distilled spirit made from the residue of the grape pressing, is surely an acquired taste but the bottles that it is put into are superbly delicate blown-glass containers of great beauty.

The list goes on. The humble light bulb is available in all manner of shapes, sizes and function. But they blow with frustrating regularity. I can expect the power to go down two or three times a week in the colder months; the ferocious electrical storms of winter increase the outages dramatically.

Italian television is a programming abomination — a banal and boring mélange of variety shows, talking heads, black-and-white Tom and Jerry cartoons and 45-year-old movies in prime time. Even pay TV stations feature 1960s films in mid-evening. One Saturday night TV special was devoted to determining whether big boobs were better than small, whether in some mysterious way they dictated the level of an Italian woman's intelligence. The notion was so bizarre that it was compulsive viewing. It could only have been screened in a nation where the macho image remains almost sacred.

In one 'event' of this boob-versus-boob bout, a small-breasted participant and a large-breasted one had to leap from a window onto an airbag dutifully inflated below by the fire brigade — good PR for the fire services — and were then awarded points according to how 'proper' their leaps were. Quite how the size of your mammary glands are a factor when jumping from a blazing building to save your life is beyond my understanding.

Another contest pitted two hapless women to determine their knowledge of Hollywood. They were escorted to a room full of remarkably accurate filmdom look-alikes — Sylvester Stalone, Elizabeth Taylor, Madonna, Christopher Reeves (in Superman tights and cape) — and had to match items with the 'stars' — a child's rubber air ring was obviously intended to be matched with the *Titanic* star while a white officer's cap was destined to sit atop *An Officer and a Gentleman*'s Richard Gere twin.

There was even a presidential-looking Bill Clinton. But where was Monica Lewinsky? Suddenly she emerged from under the table where 'Bill' was standing. It left little to the imagination to figure what she was meant to be doing to the Man . . . Another contest managed to be degrading as well as demeaning. A 'small' and a 'big' contestant sat in two glass tanks and were quizzed on various things. When one gave the wrong answer or didn't answer in time, a gush of water poured into the tank. The luckless loser was the one who received the most water, up to chest height of course.

While the show unfolded, an audience of men gazed on, scoring points from time to time as required, such as the beauty parade when small and big models paraded in a range of clothing like swimwear and underwear. At first, the 'small' contingent took a healthy points lead but gradually the 'bigs' bounced back, cutting the lead, overhauling their rivals and finally winning by a commanding majority. Small, it appears, is not necessarily beautiful in the breastworks. One can only imagine howls of outrage in more politically correct countries like America, England, even New Zealand.

Style will always win out, even on Italian television. Foreign language programmes are dubbed into Italian with seamless perfection. The dubbing skills are immeasurably better than anything I have seen elsewhere in the world.

So, too, are the shop window displays. They have great flair, beauty of presentation and taste. The windows of Siena are always a delight to pass by. Some are intricately delicate, others use simplicity to present their wares. Often they combine old and new. A tie shop, for example, may drape its products over an antique kitchen dresser or chair.

This blending of old and new extends to the towns around me with exciting effects. Modern sculpture parks and displays in the ancient cobbled alleys of tiny villages are a constant surprise. Gleaming chrome sculptures lie scattered around the streets of the historic centre of Florence like grains of salt on the black-pepper cobbles of the *piazza* and streets. At Lake Trasimeno — where motor boats, disco music and children's fairground car rides compete to be heard in the summer season — a park is dotted with towering sculptures. In San Quirico d'Orcia the carefully trimmed park within the old castle battlements is a gallery for modern Asian sculpture. One day we took some visitors to the tiny hilltop town of Montefollonico, perhaps 20 minutes away. From its walls there are sweeping views over the Valdichiana and towards the glorious San Biagio domes at Montepulciano. As we drove up through the old town gate, we were confronted by a pair of human-sized scissors jutting out from the wall. A bronzed free-standing clothes rack with metal dresses hanging from it was inside the gate entrance itself. The tiny main street was decorated with these surreal larger-than-life sculpture forms. Montefollonico was a revelation. Boasting perhaps 300 conservative souls and as old as the hill it stands on, it embraced the modern world with flair and a great sense of fun. Like the modest toothpick, it demonstrated the driving force behind the Italian soul.

Much mockery has been made of Italian driving. And yet to venture onto Italian roads is to become part of an exercise in constant vigilance and fear, a journey where anything can happen and often does. Italian drivers are not as vicious as the road rage lunatics of the Los Angeles freeway system. Nor are they as plain dumb as the German couple who drove into a river because their on-board computer system didn't tell them to stop for a ferry crossing. They are just, well, unpredictable.

On the main A1 *autostrada* that bisects Italy from north and south, even if I am driving at, say, 120 kilometres per hour, high-powered BMWs, Mercedes and Alfa Romeos roar past me as if I was parked in a roadside layby. They must be travelling at 180 kph or more. There are speed limits in Italy, but these are cheerfully ignored. There are also traffic police but they seem more intent on checking that the vehicle tax has been paid or standing around in vast numbers at accidents, looking desperately important. They are the police equivalent of a hospital rather than a preventative medicine centre.

In such a heavily policed state, the failure to police speed rules is curious. Italy and the United States rank as the most-policed countries I have ever visited. In addition to its traffic police, Italy boasts the national carabinieri, tax police, municipal police, provincial police, forest police, customs police. In my New Zealand homeland during the Great Depression of the 1930s, the Government paid unemployed men to plant what became the world's largest man-made forest. It was a wonderful job creation system. The Italian police service is a perfect parallel except it has more branches than one of the pine trees in that Kaingaroa Forest. Trees, at least, are pruned to make them grow more efficiently. I suspect in Italy they do the opposite — add more branches when the unemployment rate rises.

In the absence of a police speed prevention service on the motorways and highways, I learnt to adapt. Gradually I discovered the unwritten rules that keep the traffic moving effectively — *never* pass on the right, stay on the right unless you are overtaking, and when you have overtaken get back in the right lane as quickly as possible. In this way, you avoid having five-litre, two-tonne Mercedes monsters roaring up to you with flashing headlights and sitting a metre from your rear end until you do pull over.

Once you know these rules, the system works surprisingly well. You learn to keep an eye constantly in your rear-vision mirror checking for approaching comets. And you don't have to worry about on-coming traffic on the divided sides of the autostrada. No, Italian driving problems begin once you exit the autostrada toll booth and get out onto the roads of the towns and country.

The *slowness* of Italian driving was more of a problem. This was a quite unexpected development in my Italian education.

Italy's road system is littered with little three-wheeled

vehicles called Ape (pronounced 'Aah-pay'). They are like a measles rash — ubiquitous, ugly and a constant irritant. They are no more than motorcycles with a tiny cab for the driver and a little tray behind. They are even controlled by handlebars. They range in power from an egg-beater 50 cc to some 600 cc — these are no hog Harleys.

Overladen with an invariably old, peasant driver, and a heavy load in the tray behind, they chug, wheeze, whine and splutter on their way to market and back home. Sometimes, impossibly, both Grandad and Grandma will squeeze into the driving cabin, squashed hard into each other.

Grossly underpowered, they wheezily climb the steep hills into the old part of the towns around me. On the winding country roads, they gather a dust-cloud of following vehicles unable to pass (some drivers, driven to frustration by the snail pace, will take skin-wrinkling risks to get by them). On the busy main road to Siena, only a few cars at a time can get by them on straight stretches while a formidable line-up gathers behind them; I once counted 27 cars behind me as I waited to overtake one of these wretched little vehicles. In my 3.5-litre turbo-powered jeep with its high centre of gravity, I can envisage myself riding right on over them in a moment of road rage madness like some Italian equivalent of the Big Foot jeeps that entertain crowds at fairgrounds.

At least on that road to Siena, the slow pace allows me to 'admire' the scenery — the black African hookers who ply their sorry trade in the laybys that line the road. Like the petrol pump dispensers at the wine co-operative, they are always a highlight for visitors, a sight unseen in the countryside of New Zealand, the US or England. Women guests are even more fascinated by them than the men. They are, indeed, intriguing. Where do they come from? How do they get out into these lonely places each day? How did they get to Italy? What unkept promises were made to them? More practically, what do they charge? How many clients a day do they service? Where do they go to do their business — behind the trees, in the client's car, in a seedy room in Siena? How many passing motorists have they infected with AIDS? And how many innocents have those motorists driven on to infect?

In summer, Nancy noticed they always seem to wear something red — a crimson tight skirt, a scarlet pair of high heel shoes, sunset-red lipstick. In the damp, dank cold of winter they suffer stoically at their roadside posts.

It is a brutal and brutalising existence, at the mercy of some pimp who has no doubt taken their passports and what little money they brought with them to this 'promised' land. Certainly they would never be able to hide enough of their earnings to return to their homeland or families.

But they retain a sense of self-pride. In a season when the great Houses of Milan decided black and grey were fashionable, these pitiful young women would determinedly follow the fashion.

Only marginally better than the Ape gnats of the Siena and other roads are the equally common little Fiat Pandas. They at least look like a proper car; they even boast four wheels and a steering wheel. And on flat ground they can build up a reasonable head of steam to propel them along. But still with only a tiny motor, they huff and puff up hills at a frustrating crawl.

At the other end of the scale are the trucks. I often encounter them on the hill roads around me, carting seriously heavy loads of terracotta tiles from the factories of Petroio or the stone quarries that are weeping sores across my landscape. So heavily laden are they that their drivers have to shift down to first gear on downhill sections to stop their weight running away from them. You can imagine the speed going uphill! For these overloaded monsters, the 80 km/h speed limit for trucks is not a consideration; they would be lucky to build up to half that.

I gradually adapted to Italian road snails but I doubt that I will ever learn to live with the unpredictability of the Italian driver.

You never know when or what an Italian driver is going to do. Direction indicators are fun flashing lights on the dashboard to flick on *after* you have made a turn. Trying to second-guess a coming turn is an impossible task; a vehicle in front will suddenly slow and dart into a side road on the opposite side of the street. Motorcycles with young people appear from any side in the narrowest of alleys, both legs nonchalantly out on one side like those genteel Englishwomen on horseback in costume period films. Cars coming out of side streets blast halfway out into the road ahead; some stop when they see you, others don't bother.

In Italy, no one needs a driver's licence if their vehicle is under 150 cc. It shows. The old people are the worst. With the economic wealth now available in Italy, many of the retired people suddenly have the money to buy their own vehicle for the first time. And without the fuss and bother of getting a licence! In bureaucratic, tax-ravenous Italy, this is like a drunk getting the keys to a brewery. Like knights of old, they venture forth on their 50 cc, 100 cc or 125 cc chargers. Unlicensed, untrained and unexamined, they roam the countryside at will — like an uncontrolled and uncontrollable mob of marijuana-crazed sheep.

They seem oblivious to their surroundings, their eyes fixed with a determined gaze at some invisible spot in front of them. Their rear vision mirrors are items for personal hair styling rather than objects of road safety. They use the centre line of a road like airline pilots use the centre line of a runway — a guideline to be driven along rather than beside.

They are seriously scary.

So, too, is the life of the pedestrian. Many of the old towns around me were built before Henry Ford laid the 'miracle' of the motor car at the doorstep of the world. In these winding, narrow alleyways pedestrian and motorist compete for space. It is a no-contest battle. The pedestrian will always win.

I had been told before Nancy, Jean, Karen and I ventured into the mayhem of Rome that if a motorist and a pedestrian collide, the motorist is automatically assumed to be the guilty party. A pedestrian can thus quite safely assume a position of superiority on the footpathless roads.

I soon learned the lesson. Pedestrian crossing are places you don't bother trying to cross. The motorists ignore them and, anyway, you know that you are safe stepping out onto a roadway anywhere at all.

Pedestrians milling about on the roadside on market days are smugly confident of their survival as cars swirl around them like river water around a stone. No driver is going to be stupid enough to touch them. For all that, it is a scary business being on foot along an Italian street. Cars will scoot by just centimetres from you in some sort of game of chance. Motorcyclists swarm like the hornets of summer at San Clemente. Even the footpaths built in the newer parts of the towns often provide no refuge. Italian parking is like I imagine the universe was after the Big Bang, a chaotic mass of particles scattering haphazardly through the ether of the Italian atmosphere and coming to rest at random. The Italian attitude to parking is the perfect example of the curious contrasts in their way of life.

On the one hand, they live in a rigid world that is bureaucracy-mad, police-reigned and rule-ridden. It seems a soothing society where 'cradle to grave' welfare will provide health care, pensions and support. Form-filling is just a necessary inconvenience for these safety nets of life.

On the other hand, they can demonstrate a cavalier disdain for the rules that straitjacket their lives. They display this with cheerful abandon when they need a carpark. Any space, however small, is capable of fitting a car. If a gap between two parked cars is too small to fit another, improvise by parking at an angle into the space. Traffic will, they assume, just edge around the rear half of your vehicle jutting into the road.

If you spot a space on the opposite side of the street, simple. Just dart across and park facing the other way. Footpaths are merely a second layer of parking space behind the curbside one. Parking restriction signs are simply brightly coloured adornments on the side of buildings, pretty to look at but best to ignore. Through it all, the Italian motorist goes patiently about his business. This was another unexpected discovery. I had expected the Italian blood to show itself with arm-raising, fist-waving, wild gesticulations, road-rage gunshots, and an unceasing concerto of car horns. Nothing could be further from the truth and I feel guilt at the prejudice and assumptions I had held.

Like so many aspects of the Italian way of doing things, I learnt to live with their driving. It was a matter of survival. Returning to a more ordered country will be a difficult adjustment, I fear.

'Italian tradesmen are miracle workers,' I said to Nancy over morning coffee. 'It's a miracle if you can get them to do the work. Then it's a miracle if it works.'

She screwed up a face. 'Sounds too much like a bad joke.'

'Well, they are a bad joke,' I observed.

'This is true,' she was forced to agree.

I came to dread any dealings with the Italian 'service' industry. It was excruciatingly slow and numbingly incompetent. Our Trequanda electrician was as good an example as any. Over time, a list of repairs began to build up which I had neither the knowledge or equipment to repair — a new fitting for the light outside the kitchen door, transferring a wall cabinet with a light from one room to another, getting hidden light fittings in the upstairs library working again — simple little tasks for a qualified electrician, I thought.

No, he could not come that week for me to show him the list but yes, the next. Fair enough. Tradespeople like electricians and plumbers are in heavy demand anywhere.

So I waited. And waited. As the following week turned from Monday to Tuesday to Wednesday I called him again. 'Domani,' he assured me and sure enough the next day he came down the lane in his little white van. We walked around the house. As I pointed out the work, he studiously made notes of what to do and what new parts he would need to return with. Encouragingly, he was even able to make some repairs on the spot.

Finally he left with a promise to return the next week. Three weeks later, and after an increasing number of telephone calls, he returned. And took the same notes! He had brought no new parts with him so couldn't do any of the work. I was off to New Jersey that weekend so asked if he would come back before I left.

'E molto difficile!' he apologised with a shrug of the shoulders and outstretched arms, palms faced up.

Oh well, I resigned myself, I'll just have to wait until I return.

It took another two weeks after that before he deigned to come to do the work. Foolishly, I presumed that armed with his list and the necessary parts, he could be safely left to get on with it.

After about an hour and a half he came into the kitchen with a bill and an 'Arrivederci'. It was more with relief than thanks that I watched him disappear up the lane.

Only then did I discover that he had only done about half the work. The outside light remained unlit, as did the library lights. He had positioned the wall cabinet right above a shaving outlet, making it inoperable.

Four days later, as I sat enjoying a beer on the patio outside the Bar Paradiso, he passed by me, clearly drunk, and upbraided me for not settling the bill!

The electrician was matched by my motor mechanic in his ability to frustrate. Each time the car needed some work, it inevitably seemed to mean a stay in his workshop of at least a week, no matter the job required — the car rental people must have rubbed their hands with glee each time we came into their forecourt.

It took more than three months for him to get a small part that boosted the turbo drive for starting on cold mornings. It would have taken less, but the first part he ordered was the wrong size so he had to send for another. Meanwhile, each morning I would have to insert the faulty part into its socket, start the car, then remove it before an alarming staccato of knocks began.

One winter's night, the central heating shut down. I knew it was not a lack of oil as I had recently had the tank filled. I huddled in the kitchen, all doors shut, the burners on the gas hob alight and the oven turned up with the door open. The next morning I rang the repair people. Here I must note that service people do respond quickly when there is an emergency. Obviously, no heating in the depths of a Tuscan winter qualified because later that morning the 'lad' turned up. After fussing and fossicking for an hour or so in the boilerhouse beneath the fig tree, he succeeded in getting the boiler going, much to my grateful relief.

I should have realised it was too good to be true. Later that afternoon, as the sun set, it seized up again. Next day he came again, got it working and departed. Yes, same again — another failure a few hours later. Finally, after I had endured three nights in the cold, the old man came. He was able to get it working permanently.

The food processor gathered dust for three weeks on the shelf in the workshop of the appliance repairer. After three visits, his wife took it from the shelf and put it on the bench in front of his chair, thereby ensuring it would be the next job he faced.

The lawnmower sat forlornly on the floor of the garage for four weeks, awaiting a simple repair. Another time, the starter cord broke inside the housing. He repaired it all right, but used the same cord, which was then not long enough to give the 'oomph' to start the mower!

Then the control knob on the dishwasher broke. The repairman simply failed to show up for the first appointment. On the second he disconnected the machine and took it away in his van.

Amazingly, he returned with it the next day. This was unbelievably quick service. After one load of dishes went through, the knob came away again. He had simply glued the broken knob back into place. When the heat of the machine's hot water hit it, the glue just melted. So he had to come back with a new part. It had taken only one failed appointment and three 30-kilometre round-trip journeys from Sinalunga to San Clemente for a ten-minute job.

Repeat visits to repair places became an accepted part of our life. One day we took the television set into Sinalunga; it needed what appeared to be a minor adjustment. We arrived at the repair shop on a Tuesday morning to be greeted by a sign saying it would not open until the evening session. No matter, we took it back a couple of days later when we next went to Sinalunga. We asked if we could pick it up the following Tuesday morning when we went to the market. Sure, he said. But will you be open on Tuesday morning, we asked, conscious that he had not been the previous Tuesday.

'Si, si. Martedi mattina,' he assured us. Next Tuesday

morning, there was the sign again. 'Aperto stasera,' open this evening.

This same service establishment was later to frustrate — and bemuse — us still further. One evening, we 'lost' some of the channels available through the Italian television system. My non-technical efforts to retune the set failed, so we decided, perhaps over-optimistically given our previous experience, to call out our electrical repair shop team, which also sold TV sets and satellite dishes.

It took a couple of visits to remind them before one evening, as darkness fell, the pony-tailed younger man of the firm arrived at San Clemente in his white van. He, too, fiddled vainly with various knobs and buttons on the set before deciding that the problem clearly lay on our roof, where the aerial needed readjusting. Of course it was now dark and, anyway, he had not brought a ladder with him high enough to reach the roof. And so the first visit ended as his headlights disappeared up our lane, leaving us promises to return to sort out the problem.

Some weeks passed. We made repeated visits to the shop inquiring about the proposed timing of their return. Finally the white van reappeared one afternoon and out hopped the pony-tailed young man *and* the older one who also worked at the shop.

Despite the first visit which had pointed to the aerial as the problem, both went straight to the TV set to fiddle again . . . only to come to the same conclusion: it was the aerial, not the set. And despite that earlier visit, they had still not come with a ladder! So another hour elapsed as they explored attics to find an accessway to the roof and its errant aerial; even to our foreign eyes this seemed a waste of time — how they imagined there would be a trapdoor opening onto a tiled roof that would not leak was beyond us. And every roof around us has tiles!

Additionally, all the houses are so high that you need a particularly tall ladder to reach the roof!

And so we bade farewell again to our TV tradesmen, still channel-less but with renewed promises that they would return — with a ladder. We never saw them again. Nor did we ever receive a bill.

This performance (non-performance might be a more appropriate description) was an extreme example of the mysterious workings of the Italian tradesman. Many would arrive on jobs without the right tools, scanning our meagre toolbox for some implement that might suffice. They seem to accept that any task, however minor, is somehow fated to require at least two visits. And they have what can only be described as a cavalier attitude to payment. Some are content to wait months before payment, others ask for payment on one visit but not on others — Rocco the plumber even brought us a bottle of wine on one trek to San Clemente.

Even the high-tech world of the Internet proved depressingly treacherous. We lost count of the number of visits we made to the office of Ivan, our Internet service provider, when his system refused us access for some reason or another. In one eight-day period, we were 'down' for five days. Happily he told us that there was a message about a particular problem on his home page. It seemed futile to ask how we could get the message if his system wouldn't let us into it.

Like Ivan, they were all friendly, willing and polite. The botched jobs and return visits fazed them not at all. They seemed perfectly happy to take weeks or months to complete small repairs and certainly there was no apparent inclination to apologise.

Over time they wear you down so that you too learn to live with this particular aspect of Italian life.

❧

Italians are great starers, particularly if they sense — as they seem to be able to do with unerring accuracy — that you are a *stranieri.*

It can be an unnerving experience. They will fix their eyes on you and gaze intensely as you approach, reach and pass them by. It can last for ten or more seconds, which seems a lifetime.

There is absolutely no emotion on display during this scrutiny, no interest, no threat, no self-consciousness, no warmth, no coolness, no fear, no hatred. Absolutely nothing. Just a total, intense focus on their target.

It matters nothing if you are on foot or in your vehicle. You will still come under their gaze as you pass. No matter where they are — on the street, in a café, on a bicycle, driving a car — they can pick you out a mile off and follow your passage with this intensity of concentration.

It seems to be a gradually acquired skill as the older the person, the more intense the stare. In time I learnt to identify starers from a distance, the way their heads would turn at the sound of my approaching vehicle and stop dead — ah, a *stranieri.* I could then expect their fixed gaze to laser onto me until I had driven 100 metres or so past them, their heads slowly swivelling to keep me at the centre of their target zone.

If there is a group, all conversation will stop at my passing only to resume, presumably, when I have gone a far enough distance for them to feel 'safe' to return to their business or gossip.

I became aware of this phenomenon soon after my arrival in Tuscany.

'Have you noticed how the Italians stare at you?' I asked one expatriate.

'No,' he said. He was married to an Italian so maybe he had been granted 'stare exemption' status.

I asked another. 'No, but that's because I never look at them anyway. I did when I first arrived but the men took it as some sort of come-on signal and would follow me around the streets. So now I just look at the ground when I'm out.'

Even the dogs have become adept starers. In nearby Petroio, there is a small dog that wanders the main street in and out of the town. As we pass by, it fixes us with the same intensity of gaze as its human masters. Another sits at the entrance to the *cantina* where we buy our bulk wine on the outskirts of Trequanda. It, too, has the same concentrated gaze. When even the dogs are out on stare duty, you begin to think that this is a desperate business.

At first I became paranoid about it. Was it just me? Did I carry, unknowingly, some fearful stigmata in superstitious, Catholic Italy? Later, Nancy and other visitors were able, thankfully, to relieve me of my solitary paranoias. They, too, fell under the spell of the starers.

They reacted in different ways. Some, like me, tried to ignore them. Others would stare back. Others still would try to wave or smile. Their gestures were futile. Nothing could break the starers down. No smile, wave or return gaze could fracture their emotionless but intense stare.

In predominantly dark-haired Italy, blonde women are particularly fair 'stare game', as Nancy learnt quickly in her early visits when she had a light rinse in her hair. She came under very intense scrutiny.

What was going on behind those expressionless, intent eyes? How did they recognise a *stranieri* from so far away? What did they learn from this close inspection?

My friend Armando from the *vendemmia* at Montalcino tried to explain. He confirmed that, yes, all Italians stare.

He said that with obvious foreigners, it is because they are 'really curious'.

'They would like to talk to the foreigners but are shy and conscious of their lack of English.'

From Armando, I also learnt about the silent stare language of Italy that has a whole 'eye language' rather than a body language between men and women. A man will apparently stare at a woman he finds attractive. Depending on her interest, he will get a 'Get lost' or 'Come up and see me sometime' signal.

He told me this during one of our afternoon meetings in Siena's Irish Pub. As we talked, an attractive woman came into the bar and sat at a nearby table. While Armando chatted to me he gazed fixedly at the woman, who returned his look with the same intent gaze before returning to her book. Not a word was spoken, nor gesture made, but Armando got a message. 'She told me to fuck off,' he said.

If there is an Italian School for Starers, then most of its First Class Honours graduates must retire to Rigaiolo. This is a tiny little cluster of houses at the bottom of the hill leading up to the old part of Sinalunga. It is directly opposite the end of my lane as it spills into the Valdichiana below San Clemente. It boasts perhaps 20 or 30 houses. To my mind, it can nominate itself as the Stare Capital of the World.

Rigaiolo's population seem to be all at least 70 years old. Perhaps there is some age requirement to live there? I regularly drive through it as a short-cut up to old Sinalunga to avoid the busy main street of the newer part of town. Driving through its narrow streets — little more than lanes, really — is like running a stare gauntlet.

The old folk gather in little groups to gossip outside their homes. Here, two housewives, there three old men, over there an old woman hanging washing out of her window. Inevitably, all conversation and activity ceases as my vehicle approaches down the one-lane road that takes me into the centre, across its 'main' street and into another little lane, barely wide enough for my car, that leads to the road up to Sinalunga. It is so small that it does not even warrant a mention in the official Sinalunga guidebook while small farm complexes like L'Amorosa, with its famed restaurant, does.

It is rather like stepping into Dr Who's telephone booth. Rigaiolo feels like it has existed in this same sleepy, enclosed way for centuries, unchanged and immune from the world outside its small perimeter. Artichokes, corn and grapes grow in the fields on its outskirts. Chickens roam freely in tiny gardens. Horses graze in another field. The old women tend to their laundry and pasta. The old men sit listlessly on a stone bench under the shade of a large tree.

With my comparative youth and apparently obvious foreigner status, I feel I am the sole source of interest in their day as I pass through. Do I provide hours of gossip in my wake? Am I discussed around the dinner table at night?

Amidst this village of Honours starers, one stands out for the total commitment he brings to the task. I dub him the Champion Starer of the World.

He is a staring superstar, my man. He has a whippet-like figure. His face is like teak, weathered hard by years of working in the fields during the bitter winter cold and brutal summer sun. He sports a fine white moustache and affects an Andy Capp cloth cap. From beneath it, his eyes set upon me with the hardness of diamonds. But they carry no sparkle, just a deep intensity, utterly emotionless.

His house is the first I encounter on the little lane leading into the village. At times he adopts a strategy of height, gazing intently for staring victims from his first floor balcony chair. In summer, he prefers ground level contact and sits on the old stone bench beside the road where it meets the main street. There he waits in staring ambush, sometimes alone and sometimes with a little coterie of deputies. For fully 100 metres or more, he will fix those dark, unblinking eyes on me as I draw near. Passing, I am within perhaps half a metre from those eyes that remain riveted upon me.

I once knew a man who was involved with security at the Israeli Embassy in London. It was a particularly dangerous time as a letter bomb campaign was under way against Embassy staff and other leading Jewish figures in England. He was the first person I had met who had the 'killer's eyes' that crime novelists are fond of describing. They were hard, analytical and looked into your soul. He was a scary person.

My World Champion Starer's eyes remind me of those — pitiless, relentless and searching. What does he look for? What does he find? I have no idea.

Visitors try all manner of ploys to get just a whisper of animation or reaction from him. They try to stare him down. They wave. They smile. Their efforts are miserably hopeless and hapless against such a formidable foe. His head just swivels slowly to follow our progress. In my rear vision mirror I can see his face still fixed resolutely on me. What insight does he garner from the back of my head, I wonder?

One day as the car crawled slowly in a line of traffic at the ever-busy Sinalunga market, I spotted him on the roadside ahead. He, of course, had already spotted me and his gaze was set. As I crawled past him, his face was within centimetres of mine in the car window. It was the closest I had been to him. But still his eyes remained unfathomable, not a hint of what he might be thinking. They are like looking into a dark cavern, like the eyes of death.

The Italian shopkeeper is your enemy. He fights a guerrilla war against his customers. There are no front lines. He lies furtively behind his jungle wall of opening hours. He has no rules of engagement, no code of honour, no shopping convention of Geneva. He lays minefields of confusion. He takes no prisoners.

Make no mistake, Italian service is friendly and helpful. You just have to search for it first. The concept of open-at-all-hours corner shops, petrol stations with fast food or fresh newspapers and 24-hour supermarkets is unknown. 'Convenience' shopping is a concept the shopkeeper adopts for his own benefit; customers have to fend for themselves.

The first lesson the newcomer learns is that *everything* is closed on Sundays except the bars and cafés; in Catholic Italy, this is still the day of rest. Then you must learn to plan your shopping around the afternoon siesta, when Italy goes home or to the *trattoria* for lunch at 1 pm every day. This is one of the most difficult concepts for visitors to grasp. In natural holiday mode, they linger and tarry each morning as the retailing time bomb clock ticks down to 1 pm. At San Clemente evenings are devoted to kitchen table conversation and meal preparation so we try to accomplish our shopping in the mornings. Guests who emerge at 10 am, have breakfast and then decide to do their toilette agitate me.

Evening shopping is a venture into the unknown. Some places re-open at 4 pm, some at 5 pm, some at 5.15 pm, some at 5.30 pm. They may stay open until 7 pm, 7.30 pm, 7.45 pm or 8 pm. This question of different opening hours and days is a nightmare. Summer hours are different from autumn, winter and spring hours. Sometimes you cannot even rely on the posted hours on shop windows. The big supermarket at Sinalunga demonstrated this in the lead-up to Christmas. Normally, it is open from 8 am to 8 pm *except* Sundays (closed all day) and Mondays when, inexplicably, it opens at 2.15 pm. Before Christmas, signs told customers that it would be open on Sundays all day. So on a Sunday morning I drove the fifteen kilometres into town to get some supplies. I was greeted by a new sign announcing opening time at 2.30 pm that day.

The wine co-operative, with its silo-sized wine vats on the

outskirts of Sinalunga, is closed Sunday and Monday. Its open hours on other days are 8 am to noon and 3 pm to 5 pm.

The Bar La Siesta in Trequanda is open every day in the height of the summer tourist season but closed on Tuesdays for the other three of my seasons in Tuscany. As it is the only shop licensed to sell cigarettes in Trequanda, this can be a trap for the unwary; I have been caught short more than once.

At least Giorgio's Bar Paradiso has known hours. It seems only to open at 11 pm on Friday, Saturday and Sunday nights for most of the year, although even that cannot be guaranteed. In summer he may open at 3 pm, 5 pm or 7 pm depending, presumably, on his fancy.

Our fruit and vegetable stall is open on Tuesday and Friday mornings in Sinalunga, at the top of the town on Tuesday market day but down on the flat on Friday. If the fun fair comes in the school holidays it takes up the carpark space where the stall is set up on Fridays. Then I have to go driving the streets to find it.

The post offices in Sinalunga and Trequanda are open 8.15 am to 1.30 pm Monday to Friday but close at 12.30 pm on Saturdays. On the last day of the month they close at noon. They never reopen in the afternoon; they are a true triumph of the Italian bureaucratic system. And, like officialdom anywhere, their staff can display a rather cavalier attitude to service. In tiny Trequanda, I had become used to shopkeepers arbitrarily closing their doors at any time. The chemist might need his regular dose of 'Italian methadone' — caffeine. Fabio might decide to close up the Emporium to play a video game or two mid-morning in the Bar La Siesta next door . . . oh, well, they will be back in a moment or two, no problem. Another local at Trequanda also liked to pop into the *piazza* for a regular fix of espresso. But one day he managed to really astound me. A helping hand had been drafted into service in December to handle the pre-Christmas 'rush' (a relative term in Trequanda). One morning, I arrived to make a purchase. Doors locked, 10.30 am. Bar La Siesta, I deduced. But both of them at the same time? So I poked my head in and, sure enough, there they both were happily knocking back beers! And they were in no hurry to finish them. It was a bemusing experience, not just because of the beers but because I could not but wonder at the futility of bringing in extra help when both were going to disappear at the same time.

I have saved Enrico, the butcher, for last. He is closed from Sunday to Tuesday and opens only on Wednesday mornings. As this is where I have an account for fresh meat, I must plan my menus on Saturday to last four days before he reopens. Perversely, in summer he opens all day Wednesday and Sunday morning. The marks, shillings, pounds and guilders of the tourists are a siren-like lure. Later I learnt that he has another shop in nearby Castelmuzio, which is open on the days he locks the doors at Trequanda. He thus holds not one but two sets of villagers to retail ransom.

The 'now-you-see-me, now-you-don't' disappearing act is yet another rapid to negotiate in the river of the Italian retail world. My hairdresser at Trequanda (the only one in town) is only open on Wednesdays and Saturdays as she has other salons in the villages around that she also services. (For all intents and purposes, she is only available to me for a few hours on Saturday afternoon; those are the only hours she sets aside for men to get their locks trimmed.) She too has a two-village set-up.

One day Nancy broke her foot at her evening gym class in the little Trequanda elementary school, so we drove to the doctor's clinic in the Piazza Garibaldi — only to be forced to retrace our route and then some because that day was set aside for his clinic in Petroio.

This cross-country retailing still baffles me. In such small villages with their tiny populations, how can a shopkeeper justify running two or maybe three outlets that they man only a few days each week? Surely it makes more business sense to have one central location with only one lot of stock, one rent and power bill to pay, and one set of equipment to provide and maintain? There are, after all, regular buses plying between each of the townships so getting about is no major hardship for vehicle-less shoppers. Perhaps it is a way to write off expenses against the voracious Italian tax system? And how, I wondered, can the shopkeepers afford to simply close up shop for their annual holidays? There are plenty of them here and, by law, each worker also gets a compulsory bonus of one month's pay each year.

The butcher, the baker, the office supply maker — all simply close up at holiday time, leaving their hapless customers meat, bread and printer cartridge-less. In the case of Enrico this is a doubly cruel act because his week's holiday in fact extends through ten days. Remember, he does not open until Wednesday morning each week!

An innocent abroad might simply assume that it would be an easy matter to pop into another source of supply on days when the 'regular' shop is not open for business. Think again, buddy. In a country where bureaucracy, rules and forms are sacred icons, private enterprise takes a back seat to the gods of the public sector. Officialdom dictates what many shops can or cannot sell and charges for the privilege through a licensing system. The Bar La Siesta has the local tobacco market cornered. The petrol station is just that — a place to fill-'er-up, with nary a sniff of sweets or magazines or convenience food in sight.

But there are always the markets.

Each of the larger towns around me has a weekly market day

— Siena, Montepulciano, Montalcino, my own Sinalunga. Smaller villages like Trequanda also have their own little market days about once a month. But they are very modest affairs with perhaps a fish stall and a fruit cart set up in the *piazza*. It is to the bigger towns that the people go to market.

In Sinalunga, for example, the market day is Tuesday morning. Early in the day the vans of the vendors roll into the Piazza Garibaldi, the flat open sweep that is the heart of the old town. There are maybe a hundred of them and from them spill the goods and produce and clothes and household wares that they take from town to town each day. Quickly, the *piazza* and its little park fills. Awnings are extended over the stallholders' 'patch' from which fur coats or kitchen pans may be strung. Other vans simply have a swing-out awning cut into the side of the van; when pushed out and up like a canopy, it reveals great rounds of cheese, salamis hanging like thick, wrinkled fingers of the dead, enormous spit-roasted pigs from which slices of *porchetta* stuffed with rosemary, thyme and garlic are carved — always served cold and delicious eaten in panini bread rolls as you roam the stalls.

The fishmongers' stalls reveal slabs of pink fresh salmon, packages of the delicious mussels that still smell of the sea, translucent white squid, the small ink-black eels . . . all packed in trays of chopped ice.

The fruit and vegetable stalls offer the everyday and the exotic — artichokes, potatoes and lettuces vie for display space with pineapples from America, dates from Tunisia and kiwifruit from New Zealand.

Elsewhere, trestle tables brim with cheap plastic kitchenware or tools for home and car or corms for the garden. So laden are these tables that they threaten to topple from the gentle slipstream in my walking wake. And as I stroll, I must be wary of the perils in my path that the vendors have laid like a minefield on the cobbled stones of the *piazza* — barbecue and fireplace grills and grates, plastic dustpans and laundry baskets, garden plants and the tools to plant them.

The *piazza* is transformed, canopied almost completely with a multicoloured forest of canvas, metal and plastic. At a first, tentative glimpse it seems a labyrinth of chaos, a maze from which you might never emerge if you enter its alleys. But there is order here. Each stall has its regular assigned spot and each type of product has its assigned sector. Here are all the fruit and vegetable sellers, there are all the clothes merchants. Up there, in front of the imposingly barren façade of the church, are the sellers of hardware and tools. It is a uniformity that satisfies the need for order and rules in the archly conservative Italian psyche of rural southern Tuscany.

If vendors know their place, so too do their customers. Each week they can come to market with their shopping lists and know exactly where to go to tick off their purchases.

And come they do, in their thousands, over the five hours that the market is open. Old ladies trudge stiffly up the long, steep hill from their homes in 'modern' Sinalunga on the flat of the Valdichiana. They are hunched and bow-legged with age and arthritis. But armed with their plastic supermarket bags, they stoically endure the weekly trek to market. Villagers from nearby towns fill the blue buses that ply between them; chic, fur-clad matrons of the town's wealthier set, cool teenagers in whatever garb is the fashion of the moment.

And as they pour into the town, they bring the apparent chaos of the market to the roads. In the absence of a footpath, pedestrian marketgoers swarm onto the road itself, to be buzzed by the swarm of the traffic that swirls around them. Yet remarkably I have never seen a collision.

Some drivers demonstrate a complete contempt for their fellow motorists. One day I noticed a car parked in the centre of the post office parking area. He had successfully managed to block in about ten vehicles that had shown some courtesy (if not to post office customers) by parking nose-in around the perimeter so others could get in and out. As I walked by, a traffic warden was slapping a ticket on the miscreant's windscreen — the first-ever instance I had seen of some adherence to the rule of law in this scene of bedlam despite the presence of nonchalant carabinieri on each market day. When I returned, the motorist had just arrived back at his vehicle. Incredulous, he snatched the ticket from his windscreen, scanned it quickly and flung his arms out and head heavenward in despair. He seemed stunned and affronted to be so ill-treated by life. The fact that he had ill-treated others appeared to have passed him by in his martyrdom.

And so the hordes encircle their target before descending, Genghis Khan like, onto the surrounded encampment of the market. Its narrow passageways become a swirling, churning lifeforce. It reminds me of the maelstrom that I boated into at the base of the Canadian Falls at Niagara. Old ladies stop to gossip, banks of shoppers gather before the second-hand clothes stalls, teenagers strut and preen with the glowering, moody look of nonchalant cool; young mothers make a slow passage with their strollers, tourists stop to snap an atmospheric extra for the folks back home, their sudden then lingering attention banking up the following trail of shoppers.

On the outskirts of this rugby scrum, the old men and the farmers gather to discuss whatever it is old men and farmers like to discuss — the weather, politics, old battles, the harvest . . . not for them the indignity of shopping. While 'mother' grimly fights her way through the mayhem of the market, they hang out like weather-beaten teenagers, oblivious to the blockage they create.

The market, then, is a glorious affair for the community. It is as much a social occasion as shopping expedition, a time to catch up with old friends or make new ones, to talk and gossip, to see and be seen, to wear that new dress, to eye the girls, to escape the vines and the groves . . .

The weekly market in Sinalunga is always a rich assault on the senses. But it is as nothing compared to the Big Day in town. Once a year, the market moves downtown. Hundreds of stallholders descend from the city to join their local competitors. They come from Siena, Perugia, Arezzo and even mighty Florence. They spread through the streets of the downtown centre, under the rail underpass and into the streets on the other side of the tracks like plasma through the blood system.

They bring an avalanche of new temptations to town as well as a flood of shoppers from far and wide.

I can buy leather from Florence, salami from Montepulciano, shoes from Arezzo, wooden furniture from Perugia stained to look aged. Probably if I ventured down some back alley I could buy dope from Morocco if I was so minded. In the rail underpass, Asians and Africans squat against its walls with their pitiful displays of tawdry trash, trinkets and tinsel.

If I am in the market for clothes, the choice is enormous — knickers to nighties, silk to satin, jackets to jeans, shoes or a chemise, hankies or a hat.

Stalls try to tempt me with roasted chestnuts, hot pancakes, toffee confections and bright-striped sweets. If I need some parmesan cheese, a cheese seller will heave a 25 kg round onto his wooden block, cigarette dangling from his mouth, and use his specialist carving knives with their short blades to slice into it, much like iron wedges splitting a thick tree trunk.

If I am in the mood for a pet, I can buy a turtle or a turtle dove, a parrot, exotic birds from Africa, a goldfish with the bowl and plastic shipwreck to amuse them in their watery cage, a puppy to keep Molly company, even baby chipmunks to clear the acorns fallen from the oak trees in my woods.

I have no children here with me, but if I did I could amuse them with a toy or a helium balloon. Or I could simply send them to the Luna Park funfair that has been set up for the day.

Sinalunga's Big Day Out is a memorable one. The sights, sounds and smells of this crowded, jostling scene are like something from a history book or a Hollywood movie. But each time I go I am one of the cast of thousands, rather than a viewer in a darkened cinema.

EPILOGUE

Autumn Reprise

AS SUMMER FLOATS me like a raft on a sleepy river into my second autumn at San Clemente, familiar sight and sounds reappear to remind me that my first year in my magic kingdom is nearly over.

The crack and boom of rifle and shotgun warn me that for the next four months, violent death will once again stalk the woods and fields. The mown stalks of the chicory plants have again hardened into spears in the back lawn. The ripe figs and blackberries and grapes that weigh heavily on the tree, bush and vine tell me that this is the season for harvest.

There are other familiar sensations, too — the cooling of the nights, but days that retain their summer heat, the eerie landscape of Le Crete in the cold light of the full Tuscan moon, the glorious sunsets as the fiery ball of the sinking sun sets the sky alight, the first turning of colour in the woods of *sotto i monti* that will transform My Lady of the Mountains into a burnished swathe of gold, russet and tawny brown.

Familiar now, yes, but a familiarity that embraces me with warmth and a continuing sense of wonder.

I have a new richness in my life now — the love that Nancy and I bring to each other and to San Clemente. The anniversary of our first chance encounter in Bath has now passed, consecrated before an altar in New Jersey. Our life together in the isolation of San Clemente will no doubt be an occasional test of that love, our commitment, our character and our unity. But we look forward with a real sense of excitement to whatever course our life will take.

I have powerful memories from what has been the most astounding twelve months — the slopes of La Magia overlooking the abbey of Sant'Antimo, the feast at the truffle festival, the foot baths and mud packs of Bagno Vignoni, the beauties of Pienza, Siena and Florence, the Explosion of the Cart and the fantastic floats of Foiano, the bustle of market day, the bucket baths of summer, the pressing of the oil . . .

There are memories, too, of the people I have been lucky to encounter and friendships made or renewed with visitors from New Zealand. There are my new friends in the local *stranieri* community and, of course, my Italian connections . . . all the people who have befriended me, come to my rescue, introduced me to Italian life and its joys or simply added to the richness of my experience.

To my absentee landlord Carlo, a man of humour and tolerance for a stranger in a strange land and whom I have met only briefly during the last twelve months, I owe a special debt of thanks. He has made my year in Tuscany possible and allowed me to discover the great joys of Italy and her people.

San Clemente and Tuscany have been an inspiration in my life, but my greatest joy has come from Nancy. Our love will sustain us through the exciting years ahead.

Allan Parker
Trequanda
December 1999